THE SECRET LECTURER

An Insiders Guide to Working in a Modern University

THE SECRET LECTURER

An Insiders Guide to Working in a Modern University

PAMPHLETEER

Pamphleteer is an Australian Scholarly imprint.

First published 2016 by Australian Scholarly Publishing Pty Ltd
7 Lt Lothian St Nth, North Melbourne, Vic 3051
TEL: 03 9329 6963   FAX: 03 9329 5452
EMAIL: aspic@ozemail.com.au   WEB: scholarly.info

ISBN 978-1-925333-84-8

CONTENTS

ACKNOWLEDGEMENTS

This book was written despite my colleagues.
This one is for Adel.

PREFACE

Working at a university is one of the best jobs around.

Well, it used to be.

Today's universities are no longer what they once were. It is true that some of the worst problems have vanished, but that doesn't necessarily mean that they have gone, merely that they can't be seen anymore.[*] A lot of new problems have been created and they are easy enough to see. Whether you can or want to do anything about them is another matter. No-one wants to be seen as opposing 'progress'.

This progress largely takes two main forms. First, there is an increasing emphasis on administration. There are lots of procedures and processes which must be followed; everything must be measured and productivity objectively demonstrated.

Demonstrated: It's an interesting word which in this case is meant to mean *proven*, but *appears to be proven* might be more accurate. In the modern university perception is everything. In the absence of any real ways to measure what we do we invariably end up talking about appearances.

The second form of progress is the emphasis on teaching standards (which is another part of administration). Today's lecturer (is that even the right word anymore?) is a teacher (yes, that's much better). There is a massive amount of emphasis on get-

---

[*] Not unless you actually look. The best way of not finding any problems is to avoid looking for them.

ting the right learning objectives, transparency in marking, and other perfectly reasonable goals, but this is being done against a backdrop where most of the teaching is being done by casuals. Such casuals are often brought in at the last moment and often possessing little, if any, actual knowledge of the topic they are teaching. Their role is to keep the machine moving, get the teaching done and move on to the next subject. Teaching in a university has come to mean that you can read out the slides prepared by another lecturer, or possibly those supplied with the textbook. This is modern 'teaching'. The text-to-speech facility on your computer could do that job almost as well.

Teaching and Learning experts, and there are lot of those around, are, depending on your viewpoint, either the cause or a symptom of these problems. As such they are cruelly referred to as *education Nazis*.[*] Their job is to make sure that all the naughty lecturers are kept in line and seen to be doing the right things.

Moving on, we now have this book. After many years of rising (and falling) through the ranks in Australian Universities it struck me as odd that even though everyone was aware of the many, many problems of working in a University, it is after all the number one corridor topic, no one had thought to collate all that accumulated wisdom (and gossip) into a single, easy-to-read book. Such a book could (a) serve as an unofficial guidebook for new academics, and (b) as a reference work for established academics, struggling to work out where their careers/ lives went wrong.

It is my hope that my own pitiful example of a career (great

---

[*] If we are being pedantic (and why not?) *education Gestapo* might be slightly more accurate.

teacher + great researcher + great administrator + delusional sense of self), will help others to avoid my mistakes. It is probably too late for you, the reader, to totally escape your current fate (I'm betting you are already a lecturer or thinking about becoming one), but reading this book will keep you on the true path and, at the very least, help to stop you from leaving a meeting to find that you have (been) volunteered to do some awful job, like First Year Coordinator, Member of the Space Committee, or even worse, Head of Department.[*]

Learn the following lessons well, and keep on believing: somewhere out there, there really is a *good* university.[†]

And by the way ... all of the characters, rules, situations and other aspects of this book – except where clearly stated – are based on first-hand experience. Yes, really (YR). None of it is made up, everything that is described here actually happened, only the names (and academic disciplines) have been changed or otherwise omitted to protect the guilty.[‡]

None of the information contained here is a secret, although I suspect that most universities wish it was. I have avoided any details which might reveal either my own identify (self-preservation) or discipline (professional pride). Some universities may recognise their own stories and they are welcome to 'out themselves', but I have tried to be discrete.

Finally, I wish to acknowledge the colleagues who work in

---

[*] You have my sympathies. Once you were cool, now you are part of the hated establishment. Go ahead, tear up the Workloads, accuse the Dean of Teaching & Learning of being the Spawn of Satan (factually correct, I checked, so you cannot be sued for saying this), but no matter what you do, you will never be cool again.

[†] A time machine may be required.

[‡] I probably should have thought that through a bit more.

other universities[*] who have inadvertently helped me[†] with their own insider information. In most cases I adopted a 'I have to see that for myself' approach and have been a regular visitor to universities around the country to check out the most intriguing examples of seriously bad thinking. Or sometimes I just read their websites.

---

* Often ones I am glad I don't work for.
† They didn't know I was keeping records.

A NOTE ON SOURCES

This guide describes what it is like to work in an Australian university. Discussions with colleagues based at universities in other countries suggest that the situations there are not dissimilar. The terminology may differ from country to country (it even differs wildly within Australia), but the stories are largely the same.

In this book the term *course* is used to describe a program of study, leading to a degree in a single specified discipline (e.g., History), or faculty (e.g., Arts). A course comprises a number of *subjects*, usually referred to by their year level (e.g., a first level subject) or degree type (e.g., Master's level subject). A typical course will see full-time students completing eight subjects in each of the first three years, with some courses running to four or more years.

Other local terminology should be easily understood: workloads, subject outlines, performance appraisals, the names change from place to place, but the underlying absurdity remains constant.

1

ACCIDENTALLY ON PURPOSE

THE CAREER PATH YOU DESERVE, BUT PROBABLY NOT THE CAREER PATH YOU NEED

How and why does anyone become an academic? Clearly some form of extreme psychological trauma or pathology is a pre-requisite. All undergraduate students spend around 3–4 years of their lives, sensibly and surprisingly accurately, moaning about the uncaring, clueless teaching staff, and yet sometime between graduating and getting a job,* some of them decide instead that they want to carry on studying and to become a lecturer.

A rational person, fully informed of the facts, would never choose an academic career. Happily, the few rational people out there are rarely in possession of the facts, and so a career in academia seems a perfectly sensible choice.

Irrational people don't care about facts and so they too are perfect fodder for academia, and they will find themselves rapidly advancing to highly paid jobs such as Dean of Teaching and Learning.†

---

* It could happen!
† High pay, low status. In social gatherings, Deans of Teaching and Learning often pretend to be politicians, tabloid journalists, serial murderers, or a member of any other group with a better social standing.

Becoming an academic is rarely a deliberate choice. Instead, it is a career path chosen by those who couldn't think of a career path.*

So how do you go about getting a job at university? According to the ever-popular *Unijobs* website† you can't, because there are no jobs available. Well, there are some jobs, but none that match any degrees or training you have ever undertaken. A quick tour of the jobs' pages at each university's website is even more worrying, as after about two years of looking you realise that some universities *never* hire anyone. Perhaps the employees are all so happy they never leave, or more likely the university is staffed by Oompa-Loompas.‡

Before considering *how* to get a job at a university, we should first consider what it is that you are trying to sign up for.

THE CURRENT WORKING ENVIRONMENT

It is hard to describe the current working environment without using words that you probably shouldn't use in polite company. Basically 'We're totally f___ed', covers it pretty well, but that definitely won't do. Instead, we must look to our leaders who will describe it in the following terms.§

---

* Also note that it is a job located in some remote location and if you drive to work, which you will have to, you will pay to leave your car in the university's own car park!

† Bookmark this, you will need it. Often.

‡ If you don't know what that means you must be a Dean of Teaching and Learning. You probably missed a lot of fun things in childhood, which could explain how you ended up in your current job.

§ You can mix and match these expressions to create your own Deputy Vice Chancellor's message.

- operating in a difficult economic environment
- changes in government funding
- increasing costs
- reduced student demand.

Yep, totally f___ed.

While vast social changes are at the core of most of the current problems, many universities have contributed to this current malaise[*] by doing what is popularly known as 'shooting themselves in the foot'. The reason for this is that most universities are run by academics, who don't really understand how to run a business.[†]

Those universities that try to get round this by bringing in *real* business leaders end up with managers who don't really understand how to run a university.[‡] This is evidenced by their endless quest to improve 'quality', which is done by reducing all university activities to metrics,[§] so that changes can be documented objectively. That's what business leaders do, apparently.

Given the confusion as to the purpose of a university (to educate students, to make money?) any strategic decision-making is inherently doomed as no-one knows what the strategy is meant

---

[*] If you use clever words to describe the situation it doesn't sound nearly as bad.

[†] A university is a business. It just pretends to be something else. Didn't you get the memo?

[‡] I'm being contradictory here, but just go with the flow, it will all make sense in the end. I hope.

[§] There is a wonderful scene in the film *Dead Poet's Society* where Robin Williams rips up a textbook that shows how to measure the quality of poetry. Senior Staff from your university raided his bin and have implemented those metrics to your job!

3

to achieve.[*]

Hard to believe, I know. All those clever people (well, some of them are clever) and yet the entire university experience – if you are a staff member – is essentially a collection of random events. For example, clever, hard-working people will be declared the enemy and driven from campus. Meanwhile others, with a personality so toxic that all the clever, hard-working people quit just to get away from them, will find themselves spoken of as 'the very soul of the university'.[†] The toxic staff are left behind, since no other university in their right mind[‡] would ever hire them, and 'being left-on-the-shelf', is mistaken for loyalty. Dr Toxic, with cockroach-like survival skills, will find some nice faculty-level admin job and never leave. They truly are the soul of the modern university.

The random nature of university life can be further illustrated with the following cautionary tales.

A CAUTIONARY TALE

There once was a university that employed admin officers, one per department, to help staff with processing their expenses claims and purchasing requests. This large number of staff cost the university a lot of money and so a new computerised expenses' system was installed.

---

[*] It's a bit like trying to decide whether a jury has done a good job. Did they give the right verdict? What was the *right* verdict?

[†] I know of one case where a new staff member resigned on their first day of work after discovering that they had been hired along with the toxic person they had been trying to escape from at their previous employer.

[‡] I get the irony of that sentence.

- This system cost a lot of money.
- Installing the new software crashed the university network (several times).
- Lots of admin officers were reassigned to other jobs, but many were 'let go'.

Still, it was all worth it as the new system would be more efficient and 'save money'.

Except it didn't do either.

The system was hopeless. It was impossible to use and staff couldn't get their expenses processed, so the university came up with a solution: hire admin officers (one per department) to help the academic staff to enter their expenses. Brilliant!*

The funniest part of the above tale is that the company who supplied the software didn't even use it themselves, using software provided by yet another company.†

ANOTHER CAUTIONARY TALE

There was once another university (or possibly the same one) that wanted to improve its email software. Two rival companies made bids for the contract.

The first one offered software that was easy to install, easy to use, extremely cheap and gave each staff member several GB of space for holding all their emails.

The second one offered software that was hard to install (a complete system overhaul was required), hard to use (configuring each computer had to be done manually by a tech expert),

---

* In a university for every one step forward, two steps are taken back.

† Go on, you try to make up this sort of stuff.

unbelievably expensive (of course), and offered staff enough GBs of storage space to store every photo of their cats that they had ever taken.

Guess which one the university chose?

Rumour[*] has it that one of the senior staff in charge of choosing the new system was from the arts faculty, where staff[†] routinely email each other huge files as attachments[‡] and they needed vast storage space for their emails.

CHOOSING YOUR FIRST EMPLOYER

Chances are your first job will be at the university where you did your postgraduate study, which will be the same one as where you did your undergraduate study. This often explains why so many staff are so clueless: they have only ever experienced one way of doing things (probably badly) and think it's normal.

Universities come in lots of different shapes and sizes, but these can be readily classified into one of three main groupings.

At the top, you have your elite universities. These typically have a beautiful sandstone (or even better) campus, a vibrant campus life, a café or bar that is actually open in the evening, possibly a few Nobel Prize-winning staff, multiple five-star research rankings, and they only let in the top 10% of school leavers.

At the bottom, you have your regional universities, or those located in the part of a big city that no-one sensible ever goes to. These typically have unpainted prefabricated buildings with as-

---

[*] Corridor gossip at a university can always be relied on to be accurate.

[†] All four of them!

[‡] Probably artistic pictures of cats.

bestos in the ceilings,* a kiosk where you can get coffee between 9 and 2 (Monday to Friday only), a bar that closed in 1995 when alcohol on campus was banned, staff about one year older than the average graduating student, and they accept school leavers if they avoided being in the bottom 10% of their year.†

In the middle of all that you have your middle-ranking universities, who are driven by a desire to either break into the elite upper grouping (which is never going to happen but everyone likes a trier), or a desire to avoid being lumped in with all the grubby regional/inner-city universities. Many of the more deluded middle-rankers, particularly those stuck in regional areas (a fact that is pretty hard to keep hidden), attempt to *differentiate themselves*‡ by emphasising some particular skill or unique feature.

The existence of this point of differentiation is usually sprung on unsuspecting staff at the launch of the university's latest accounts, which will be described as 'challenging' or some other evasive way of saying 'bad'.§ But don't worry, the accounts are likely to be accompanied by the latest version of the university's *Strategic Plan* which is the path to ultimate salvation. This plan, which will be short on actual detail (but with lots of very nice stock images), will identify the few remaining parts of the university that still have some decent staff, and set out a strategy to

---

* It may also have an exit door on the third floor that doesn't have any stairs under it (I could name the building, campus & university, but won't).

† Obviously, exceptions can be made for the right candidates.

‡ Told you, if you use clever words things don't sound so grim ... or desperate.

§ Although such documents are very boring, they are always worth reading. Check out the bonuses your Senior Staff get for meeting totally unspecified performance targets. You didn't know they got those, did you? Why don't you get a bonus? See, told you that you should read them.

'be more like those people'. As you can see, strategic planning at a university is a very complex process and performance bonuses are fully justified.[*]

The other parts of the strategic plan can be summarised as follows: If your department has either (a) lots of students, or (b) lots of grants, chances are the staff will still have a job this time next year. If your department has falling student enrolments, a research ranking of 'n/a',[†] then you might want to start thinking about tidying up your CV. Alternatively, if you are the toxic lecturer in your department, see what faculty-level admin roles are on offer.

When you get a job at a university you are probably replacing another member of staff who has left. Note that when you start it is often the case that no one will tell you what happened to your predecessor. Did they retire after a long and distinguished career? Did they get another job? Did they just go home one Friday evening and never come back again?[‡] No one will say.

Occasionally, and only occasionally, you might land a *new* position. This probably means that your new department is highly successful, and your position is part of their expansion and plans to dominate the market.[§] Or, it is more likely that the latest accreditation report revealed that they have been massively under-staffed for a decade and someone has finally noticed.

---

[*] It might be worth mentioning this at your next staff meeting when your Head tells you that the Department budget has been cut by 50%.

[†] The polite way of saying zero, but with a thinly veiled suggestion that 'OK, it looks bad, but we have an excuse. Honestly we do.'

[‡] This happens a lot more often than you would think. None of the remaining staff want to appear insensitive and so no-one ever asks 'Where is ...?'

[§] It could happen.

SO WHAT DO YOU DO AROUND HERE?

There are lots of different academic jobs at a university, starting at the bottom with the role of tutor, where you are a hybrid of postgraduate student and lecturer; through to the top where you find the Senior Staff, who are a hybrid of business manager and snake.[*]

Let's take a look at these various roles.

TUTOR

A tutor is usually a postgraduate student who needs money (are there any who don't?). These staff will be experts in their teaching fields by virtue of having 'done well' in the subject as an undergraduate. A scraped Distinction (see *Grading*) from two years ago now becomes the qualification that will earn the student an entry-level teaching job.

Despite the fact that by spending all their time 'teaching', that their own PhD will never get finished, tutors show excessive eagerness to take on any type and amount of teaching. At regional universities, where there are no longer any real staff left,[†] a tutor may be put in charge of running an entire subject: all the lectures, tutorials, marking and administration.[‡] For all that effort they will be paid about one-tenth of the salary an actual lecturer

---

[*] This is just plain rude: associating Senior Staff with snakes is grossly unfair. Sorry, snakes.

[†] Apart from the toxic one, and those on their way to interviews with other employers.

[‡] If you have never seen this happening, then you are at a real university. You should get out more and see how the other half lives.

would have cost the university to do exactly the same task.*

No wonder there are so many tutors at university.

Tutors are usually young, very likable, and have absolutely no idea what they are doing. However, the feeling of self-importance from being a tutor and the small trickle of income make them think they are living the good life!

TEACHING FELLOW

While slavery has been abolished in most civilised countries, it is still practised in some uncivilised locations, such as Australian universities. Teaching Fellows are usually former tutors who still haven't got round to finishing their PhD, but can talk-the-talk sufficiently well enough to make it sound like they are on their way to completion.† Desperate for a job, they accept the job of Teaching Fellow, which will allow them to finish their PhD while they get some teaching experience. Only one of those last two statements is true.

LECTURER

Lecturers are employed to teach, do some research and some admin. As they are new to lecturing, the admin roles they are given are usually unimportant and of no real consequence, say 'year coordinator'. Such jobs sound important, but if you don't do it no-one will notice.‡

----

* Now that's how to run a business.

† They may even have completed their data collection phase. Obviously, they won't have written anything yet, but they will. Honest.

‡ As Head I once asked a colleague whether he would agree to continue his role as second-year coordinator. He said he didn't know he was the

The expectations on research are equally non-descript. Yes, you are expected to do some research, but the reading-between-the-lines here says: try to publish parts of your newly completed PhD. Don't even think about starting anything new.

The teaching role is far more concrete. Assuming that the Teaching Fellow is already busy,[*] a new lecturer can expect to be given first-year teaching.[†] This means dealing with large classes of students who are so clueless that they can't find their lecture theatre on a map.[‡] Having absolutely no idea that they are being overworked, lecturers actually volunteer for additional teaching duties and will even offer to give talks to Year 12 school students thinking about going to university. They are so keen it is plain scary.

Lecturers do all this because they think this positive attitude will be noticed and they will be promoted to Senior Lecturer.

It won't, and they won't (respectively).

SENIOR LECTURER

Senior Lecturers are the lifeblood of a university. They do most of the important teaching and with their years of experience, they know how to get things done, who to talk to when there's a prob-

---

second-year coordinator; he thought he was the third-year coordinator. He never did anything in that role so he didn't mind volunteering to do it all again the next year.

[*] A relative term. Here it means 'already teaching more weekly face-to-face hours than there are number of hours in the working week'.

[†] Or any other teaching that the Senior Lecturers managed to avoid. Think of being given first year teaching as a kind of hazing ritual.

[‡] Even when they are standing outside the building, which has a giant sign on it with the building name and number. Oh yes, been there, seen that.

lem, which rules can be bent, and which rules can be broken.

As such, they are universally despised by Senior Staff.

To Senior Staff, a Senior Lecturer is a disgruntled employee who was turned down for promotion to Associate Professor: all the trouble in the university is caused by Senior Lecturers, what with all their rule bending and breaking.

Senior Lecturers actually care about their students, and their research. They basically like what they do for a living and aren't planning on going anywhere anytime soon. The tragic realisation that their employer has not even noticed their hard work, but that every mistake (real or imagined) has been fully recorded, can leave dreams of being promoted *on merit* to Associate Professor in shatters. Instead, the only way up for a Senior Lecturer is to move university. It's far quicker and easier[*] to get a better job with a bunch of complete strangers than it is to convince the people you have been with for years that you are actually damned good at your job.

ASSOCIATE PROFESSOR

An Associate Professor is a Senior Lecturer who escaped from one university, and has been rewarded with a promotion at another. They spend most of their time explaining to people that they are part of the *Professoriate*, because the term 'Associate Professor' doesn't seem to mean anything to anyone outside a University.[†]

---

[*] For example, to get a new job you send a cover letter, reply to selection criteria and a CV. To get promoted you do all that as well, but it has to be written in blood.

[†] It actually confuses a lot of people in universities. I know one university where all Associate Professors have 'Dr' on their door and staff webpages, presumably because the university itself doesn't recognise the ranking.

Associate Professors are, or rather were, very good at research and even better at making people think they are/were good at teaching. Their main skill is that they have spotted how to play the system, for example, knowing which students are the class opinion-leaders and making sure that they always get lots of attention in class* and of course, suitably high grades.

Associate Professors are basically Senior Lecturers gone bad. Every rule that can be bent or broken will get bent or broken, but only when no-one is looking. A devious and cunning mob, you could learn a lot from them.

PROFESSOR

A Professor is a senior and respected member of staff who is an acknowledged world leader in their field. The Senior Staff seek the wise guidance of these experts and shape university policy and strategy around their input.

Just kidding.

Professors are indeed experts, that much is rarely in any doubt. The trouble is that as far as their own university is concerned they are interfering so-and-sos, who don't seem to realise that their job is to stand around 'being inspirational' and that no-one wants to hear what they have to say about anything. For example, your average Professor† might point out that cutting staff numbers and increasing the student intake will end badly for all concerned. This will be dismissed as

---

* Or which ones to take for coffee.

† There's no such thing as an average Professor, they are all 'above average'. Hang on, how is that even possible? They can't *all* be above average? Well they are, so get over it.

'yet another example of the distinguished Professor failing to understand the current economic situation'.

As a consequence, Professors spend large parts of the day staring at their projected Superannuation accounts, trying to calculate the optimum moment to retire.

DEAN

Deans[*] are living proof of the *Peter Principle*[†] in that they have reached their maximum level of incompetence. Part of their inevitable bitterness (they hate all their staff, apart from a few randomly[‡] chosen 'lucky ones'), stems from unrealised dreams of breaking through to some Deputy Vice Chancellor job (see *Senior Staff*), or possibly even, dare we say, the top job itself.

So how do Dean's get stuck in this role? Once upon a time your average Dean[§] was a Head of Department, or possibly the Head of a Research Team and by and large, they were making a good job of it: keeping everyone in their Department or team happy and productive. Their excellent work (or if we are being honest, luck) then got them the job of Dean. Now they have absolutely no idea what they are doing: they have reached their point of maximum incompetence. How come? Well, basically a Dean is a person put in charge of multiple teams, most from out-

[*] The title varies from university to university. Here, the term Dean refers to the person above the Heads of Department, but below the various Vice-Chancellors. You know, your basic middle manager.

[†] Look it up. It will explain why all universities are so badly run.

[‡] Talent has nothing to do with it: it's usually Dr Toxic. Deans latch on to those they perceive as competent and no contradictory evidence will shake that perception.

[§] And they are all *average* … at best. Sorry, I promise I won't do this again.

side their own area of expertise, and operating on an ever-shrinking budget. Put it like that and you might have a small spark of sympathy for Deans. Don't be fooled. They are totally beyond any human feelings and should be avoided at all costs. Deans operate on the principle that everything you say or do will be recorded and will be used as evidence *against* you.

One simple way to bring Deans back to earth would be to actually make them do some teaching. The obvious solution here is that they teach in the discipline they originally trained in, possibly even in an area in which they have some expertise.* But that would completely miss the point. Deans operate on the belief that all lecturers are essentially inter-changeable, and of course replaceable. So, the best thing to do here would be to have the Dean take charge of a randomly picked subject, and in a randomly picked discipline. And this subject would change every year. They can hardly complain about this process as it's the same one that all their staff must adhere to, and as for them being too busy, well that's nonsense, teaching is only a few hours on a Workload.

THE SENIOR STAFF

This comprises the Vice-Chancellor (your boss!) and all the various underlings that also have the words 'Vice-Chancellor' in their job title. Starting with the obvious ones, this includes the

---

* Some Deans do 'teach'. That is, they give a guest lecture on the topic they are an expert in. In conversation they will make it sound as if they taught the entire subject. Sometimes the Dean will give a research talk (expect to hear about studies they did 20 years ago), or a talk on 'leadership', which will be based on whatever management article they just found on the internet.

Deputy Vice-Chancellor,[*] Pro-Vice Chancellor,[†] Senior Deputy Vice Chancellor,[‡] and sometimes a 'Vice President'.[§]

After all those senior staff come the Pro-Vice Chancellors in charge of specific faculties, campuses, or something called 'Engagement'.[¶] A university may have between 10 and 20 senior staff.

Chances are you will never meet any of them.

Should the unlikely happen, probably after accidentally wandering through the wrong building, you may happen to bump into one of these Senior Staff in the corridor (they are easy to identify: they wear a suit) and they may speak to you. You should always offer a brief explanation as to why you are not currently engaged in face-to-face teaching.[**] Under no circumstances should you ask them any questions, like 'So what does a Deputy Vice-Chancellor (Engagement) do?'.

The correct etiquette for dealing with senior staff can be illustrated with the following story.

I once bumped into a suit in the corridor and they asked me who I was and something almost (but not quite) like a conversation started. Fortunately, a colleague, who had been at the university forever, arrived and identified me to the suit. After the

---

[*] Fair enough, having a Deputy is logical.

[†] Often the real Deputy, but with a cooler job title.

[‡] There are often lots of Deputies, which gives someone an excuse to create a very pretty chart showing the university's organisational hierarchy. Even the Deputies have to check this regularly to see who they are supposed to lead, and who to follow.

[§] No one knows what this person does, but their salary is a lot higher than yours. Plus they get performance bonuses.

[¶] Again, no one knows what this person does either.

[**] Always say you are on your way to a lecture.

suit left I asked my colleague why they hadn't identified the other person to me? The response I got was: 'God does not need an introduction'.

The chances of you actually ever speaking to a member of senior staff are slim. They only emerge from their offices when the Vice-Chancellor (or possibly a Deputy) gives the latest status update, which usually centres on naming a list of disciplines that are no longer going to be with us. In such circumstances, keep out of sight, or they may start thinking about your discipline.

You are advised to think of Senior Staff as Monty Burns-types,[*] who will happily nod as you speak to them, whilst they are discretely pushing a button to summon the hounds.

MEET THE STUDENTS

In the past, lecturers were advised to think of students as future colleagues. This variant of the *Golden Rule*[†] would ensure that students were treated with respect and professionalism.

Today, staff are better advised to think of students as future opponents in a court case.

The modern student clearly differs in many ways from their predecessor. Learning issues[‡] are one aspect of these changes, but the fundamental difference, the one that most modern lecturers don't get is this: many of the students don't want to be there.

Long ago most students *wanted* to go to university, they knew

---

[*] Who? You really are a Dean of T & L aren't you?

[†] Another one to look up.

[‡] Like the modern student having an attention span that can barely be measured in nanoseconds.

what they were getting themselves into and putting some effort into learning was an accepted part of the process. Hard work would be rewarded in a reasonably linear relationship, sufficient to keep everyone suitably motivated.

Today, many students aren't sure why they are at university. They know they are *supposed* to be there, but that's not the same as *why*. A degree is no guarantee of getting a job, let alone one that will pay enough to mean that the student debt taxation will start to kick in.[*]

Consequently, many sleepwalk through degrees, with a focus on doing what is required to get through each subject, rather than what they might learn. In practical terms, if it isn't assessed, it isn't going to be studied.

While this is clearly true of the great masses, even the very best students see strategic studying as part of getting the best possible degree grade.[†] Subjects will be chosen based on the assessment type and perceived difficulty. Lectures and tutorials attended only if the cost-benefit analysis is positive.

Overall, most of the students you meet will be honest, pleasant and fairly[‡] hard working. However, the 80:20 rule applies very well here in that 80% of your problems will come from only 20% of your students.

---

[*] What a cheering prospect that is: get a degree, get a good job, get a big tax bill.

[†] There's nothing inherently wrong with this, and in many ways this approach reflects a high level of strategic decision making (probably a good thing). It is, however, cold and functional. Wonder why attendances are falling? One answer (there are many): there's no fun at university anymore.

[‡] Let's not get too gushy.

2

WELCOME TO THE JUNGLE

THEN AND NOW

Having got your PhD, and done all the most important status updates,* it is time to get down to real work. Many years ago a new academic would be eased into their lecturing role, with a very light teaching load in their first semester, possibly only 2–3 lectures in areas linked to their own research, all done under the careful stewardship of an experienced member of staff. Additional lectures and the coordination of whole subjects would be gradually introduced over the next semester.

Today, a lecturer can expect to teach 2–3 entire subjects in their first semester.† That should get them warmed up before things get really busy. There is no mentoring, although if you do need clues as to what you are supposed to be doing, you can read the subject outlines of your predecessor (*see Subject outlines*). The chances of any of these subjects having anything whatsoever to do with your research background is somewhere between slim and none. All new lecturers are deemed to be inter-changeable within their discipline and will be expected to go wherever the

---

* For example, making sure your credit and loyalty cards say 'Dr'.

† Guaranteed if they are hired at the rank of Teaching Fellow or Lecturer.

need arises (see *The Dean*).

MEET AND GREET

The first thing you will notice on starting your new job is that most of your colleagues either do not exist,[*] or at least they don't seem to come into work anymore. Should you happen to see someone in your corridor, they will not introduce themselves, so it's hard to be sure.

The best way to find out your colleagues' names is to watch who goes into which office. After a period of about a week you should be able to make some reasonable guesses as to identities by linking movements to the name plaques on the doors. This is not always a reliable strategy though, so loitering outside offices and listening in when the phone rings might be helpful.[†]

If you are very unlucky you will be introduced to your colleagues at a staff meeting. Your colleagues will give only the most limited descriptions of themselves, usually just name, rank and the subjects they teach.

REPLY ALL

Despite their physical absence, you will probably be able to develop a reasonable working profile of most staff members by following the email chatter in your Department. For example, if a member of staff is given a prestigious new administrative role,

---

[*] They don't exist. The modern university has more admin staff than academic staff, and most of the academic staff are casuals.

[†] At the very least it will give you 50% of the skill-set required to be a Head of Department.

such as First Year Coordinator, and this is publicly announced by the Head of Department,[*] several working profiles can be generated.

First, the Head of Department is a sadistic so-and-so who not only hands out terrible jobs, but insists on publicly humiliating the poor recipient. Bad Head!

Second, the recipient, who is probably a junior member of staff, is naïve for having been in the wrong place at the wrong time when that job was handed out.

Third, the first person who commits the sin (and it's a big one) of hitting 'Reply all' to offer 'Congratulations' on that appointment can be profiled as the Department's Dr Toxic. It's one thing to see a colleague suffering, quite another to openly gloat about it.

Fourth, the person who hits 'Reply all' after that initial congratulation, is terrified of Dr Toxic and wants to keep in their good books.

Fifth, the name of everyone who doesn't send an email should be noted. These are probably the good members of staff and the reason they didn't group reply to the email is because they have already taken the new First Year Coordinator out for a few commiserative drinks.[†] They didn't invite the Head of Department and they certainly didn't announce it in an email.

---

[*] The more congratulatory the email the more trivial and stupid the job is likely to be. Really interesting news like a staff member winning a $50,000 grant will never be mentioned. It would just upset the other staff.

[†] When I was made Head of Department I kept a record of the number of emails saying either congratulations or commiserations. It was a tie. The ones who offered commiserations helped me every time I asked, the senders of the congratulatory messages were always busy. There's probably some important higher truth in that story. Beats me what it is.

AN OFFICE JOB

The learning-of-names ritual will probably take about 2 months before you can name all of your colleagues. The reason staff don't use their offices, apart from having new staff members and the Head of Department loitering outside, is because it is impossible to work there. The constant stream of whining, aggressive, manipulative visitors makes it impossible to concentrate. It's even worse when the students start coming as well.[*]

The other drawback of using your office, is that if people know where to find you then they will ask you to do *things* …

Things you don't really want to do … especially if you are a new member of staff and haven't yet realised that being asked to join a committee is never an honour (see *Administration*). What you need to realise is that your Head of Department will delegate tasks[†] based on the very fair principle of 'first person I see'. If you do not have an invisibility cloak, the next best thing is to keep away from your office.[‡]

PERSONALISING YOUR OFFICE

Most of your first few days at work will be spent customising your office. Various tech people will arrive to get your PC up and running,[§] which is all fine and good. The tech people want to be

[*] Sorry. Couldn't resist it.

[†] That is, anything boring that they don't want to do.

[‡] If cornered about your apparent absence from work, claim that you were working in the library. Say it with a straight face and chances are no one will call your bluff.

[§] It is advised that you tell the tech person that you want to use the

your friends and as they have downloaded every pirated movie and TV show ever made, and have them stashed on the university hard drive,[*] it's going to be the beginning of a beautiful friendship. Unfortunately, they have also downloaded every porn movie ever made, so be careful about watching anything they give you whilst at work.[†]

Some days later someone will come to set up your phone. They may try ringing you first and as they are the only people who know your new number, you will be so intrigued that you may actually answer the phone.

Never do this again.

If people think you can be reached by phone, then you will find yourself being asked to do even more *things*, usually *urgent things* so whatever you are doing will have to be dropped in favour of this new mission.

Even though it will be university policy, under no circumstances should you create a voicemail message (don't even record your name!). If you create one, and people hear it, apart from thinking you sound very tinny, they will know that they have reached the right phone extension and expect you to return calls.

Never return calls. If it is important[‡] they will send an email.

---

computer to play games. They will understand and provide you with a machine that's so powerful that it could be classified as 'alive'. Saying the PC is for email and writing lectures will get you a second-hand slab of metal that makes clunking noises when you turn it on, or possibly a Mac. Serves you right.

[*] This is true of every university.

[†] Your Head of Department will probably be outside your office.

[‡] It won't be. It's a university, nothing that you could honestly describe as *important* happens here. If it was important it would be happening somewhere else.

Once all the tech stuff is done the real work of customising your office can get going and you can unpack the ten books you currently own. They will look pitiful and lost there on the four rows of (cheap) bookshelves that run around your walls. [*] Don't worry, within a year or two all the shelves will be filled with textbooks that you didn't order and your office will look suitably academic.

Posters, prints or paintings can be put on the walls. These will reflect your (a) personality, (b) tastes, and (c) how cheap you are (posters were fine in your student room, not in an office).

Putting up a print (or poster if you have to) featuring a popular modern band, say *The Rolling Stones,*[†] will give you plenty of kudos with ... yourself. Everyone else will think you are a dinosaur.

Prints depicting a 1927 Paris art show (did you go?), or a furry tapestry, can be hung tastefully from most walls, provided the plasterboard walls can take the weight.[‡]

Never, under any circumstances, should you put up your degree certificates. This will irritate visitors (both students and staff) who will think you are showing off. In theory your colleagues should have similar degrees, but probably don't.[§] The

---

[*] Even though they look like they will collapse under the weight of two paperbacks, these shelves can withstand earthquakes and will still be there long after you are gone.

[†] This can only be done by 'cool' Associate Professors. If you are neither, don't do it.

[‡] You aren't supposed to put nails in your office wall. Do it anyway, it's not as if anyone will ever check, and if they do, hide the hammer and say they were there when you arrived.

[§] Those ranked at Lecturer or higher should have degrees (plural), but this depends on your discipline. Some will have 'professional qualifications' which can be roughly translated as 'No PhD'.

students will not see your degrees as aspirational targets,[*] but as several more years of their life and a student debt edging ever closer to six figures.[†]

You may also add furniture to your room, an old sofa is usually acceptable, as are potted plants (real ones, not fakes). If you have young children, you may also add a box of toys and set up a small table for doing drawings or playing with an iPad. You will need these during school holidays when you have to bring your children onto campus. Universities are very tolerant of noisy creatures running around screaming and throwing things. They have to be, otherwise all the Senior Lecturers would be out of a job.

THE UNIVERSITY WEBSITE

Your university has a website.

You are not on it. Don't believe me? Go check. Follow the links, don't use the search facility. That's cheating.

Ok, did you find your entry? Did you find your Department? Your Faculty?

The (probable) answer to all these questions is 'No'. If you answered 'Yes' to any question, then you are probably at a 'real university',[‡] you know, one where they still have a budget[§] and standards.[¶]

---

[*] You thought you were going to be a source of 'inspiration' for your students? That's so cute.

[†] I told you no rational person would become a lecturer. No rational person would even do a degree.

[‡] As believable as Hogwarts.

[§] One that is in the black, obviously.

[¶] Don't worry about this word. It has nothing to do with you. Please move

If you want to get on your university Website, you must first track down the person responsible for editing content. This person will have left the university and so you will next need to identify the person who is *going to* edit the content. When you have identified that person, and been surprised to discover that it is you,[*] you will need to sign up for the web editing course on offer at your university. The next one will be scheduled for March … next year.

Given the apparent impossibility of updating web pages, particularly with the constant restructuring that goes on at universities where your department shifts from School to School, College to College, or Faculty to Faculty,[†] many universities have opted for a cleaner more streamlined look. This is one where there are no staff pages, no department pages, and the university Twitter feed dominates the home page.

---

along to the next paragraph.

[*] To make up for not paying anyone to edit web pages, universities have now empowered staff to edit their own web pages. Except staff are not allowed to use the web content manager (they might break the Internet) so nothing ever gets updated.

[†] I am certain that one day my entire department will wake up to discover that we have all changed discipline, and university. Actually, I think that has already happened, it's hard to be sure.

3

THE 40:40:20

EIGHT DAYS A WEEK

When you are a lecturer you will be given a *Workload* document. This Workload serves many purposes. For the staff member it is a contract showing that their work will not be unfairly taxing. This is a lie.

For a Head of Department, it is a way of ensuring all teaching obligations are met and ensure the fair allocation of tasks. This is also a lie.

For Senior Staff it is a way of forcing all those lazy lecturers to do more and more teaching. This is not a lie.

Your Workload document should be constructed with your input at the start of each academic year. In reality the Head of Department will throw it together in secret sometime after the first semester has started (week 3 is the modal value)[*] and you will learn that for the last couple of weeks you missed the lectures you were supposed to give in a subject you were previously unaware of even existing. Your Head will casually tell you that they have already had several complaints about the lecturer's no-shows, and that you can expect your teaching evaluations to be

---

[*] It's semester 1 week 11 at my university and we still haven't done ours.

lousy, but not to worry,[*] as they understand the difficult position you have been put in.[†]

Workloads are typically separated into three parts: teaching, research and administration These parts are each allocated a percentage weighting, such that your role might be described as 40:40:20, or something similar. This means that 40% of your time (or two days per week) will be spent teaching, 40% (two days) doing research and 20% (one day) on admin. In no way does this reflect any form of reality. A more accurate role description would be: 80:0:40.

Research (see *Research*) is what you do at weekends, once you have caught up on your teaching and admin backlogs. Alternatively, research is something your postgraduate students do, and you try to take credit for.

'WHEN YOU ASSUME, YOU MAKE AN ASS OUT OF U AND ME'

The Workload calculations are based on a series of *assumptions* about (a) how many working hours there are in a year, and (b) how long it really[‡] takes to get a job done. For example, let's assume you have 5 weeks of holiday (universities are good on holidays), so that means you work 47 weeks per year. The working day is about 7.25[§] hours, so the Workload assumes that you are working for 47 (weeks) x 5 (days per week) x 7.25 hours = 1703.75 hours per year. This figure is then used to calculate

---

[*] The entire content of this conversation will be forgotten when the teaching evaluations come in.

[†] They understand because they put you in it.

[‡] Not really.

[§] There's some variation on this point (range 7–18 hours per day).

the hours you should be involved in each task, such as 40% of 1703.75 = 681.5 hours of teaching.

That almost sounds logical. It's what happens next that causes all the heartache. Let's assume you are going to teach 681.5 hours per year.[*] Given that the typical university semester is 13 weeks long, and there are (surprise, surprise), two semesters, then there are 26 teaching weeks. This means that in an average in-semester week you could be asked to do just over 26 hours of teaching (i.e., 681.5/26).

Fortunately, attempts at some universities to actually implement that particular interpretation of Workloads have largely disappeared, although a few still remain. In such cases the Senior Staff at the university will defend the Workload by pointing out that there is no teaching for 21 weeks of the year, or that the average teaching hours per week across the year (47 weeks[†]) are only 14.5 hours. At this point the Senior Staff will compare these hours to those worked by a school teacher, to show how utterly unreasonable staff are to complain about being made to do even the smallest amounts of work.

Confronted with staff complaining that 'lectures don't write themselves',[‡] other universities have made allowances for preparation time and each actual hour of standing in front of students (i.e., 'face-to-face teaching') is given some associated preparation hours on the Workload calculations. This means that one hour of teaching will be allocated a few hours of preparation time,

---

[*] No one can admit the essential silliness of these calculations and so there is no rounding. Workloads are invariably calculated to several decimal places.

[†] Or 52 if they are particularly devious.

[‡] Sadly, not true. Lectures do write themselves, see *Teaching*.

say three extra Workload hours. Tutorials (see *Tutorials*), which are deemed to be easier to do than lectures might get an hour of preparation time to go with the actual hour of face-to-face time.

The teaching Workload then gets even more complicated as hours are allocated for marking, creating new subjects, managing large classes, implementing new teaching delivery methods, and so on. By now, as you can imagine, the Workload, which is calculated on a spreadsheet,* would defy interpretation by the entire mathematics department (if you've still got one of those).

All that really matters – as far as your Head of Department is concerned – is that your teaching Workload hours match the specified target hours, say 651.5 hours.

If your total is less than the target (say 651.0 hours), then you will be allocated more teaching.

If your total exceeds the target, then your teaching load will … be … reduced …

…

Sorry, small technical glitch there. I had to have a long lay-down after writing that. That never happens. If your Workload exceeds the target you will just have to do it as 'the budget is very tight this year'.†

---

* The spreadsheet never works, so some universities prefer to do all these calculations with a handwritten document. That one detail will tell you a lot about your university.

† So tight that some universities have stopped hiring cleaners to clean lecturers' offices. Paper bins in offices have been removed and as far as I can tell from the absence of any communal bin near my office, staff are expected to take their rubbish home with them.

MYTHICAL BEASTS

There are many urban legends about some staff being given a 'research focussed' position, but like all urban legends there is no factual basis to any such claims. The only truly research focussed positions carry titles like 'Research Fellow', not 'Lecturer', and they only stay research focussed until the Head of Department decides that the Research Fellow doesn't seem to be doing anything, and gives them a subject or two to teach.

There are quite a few 'administration focussed' roles, and while these too are subject to many myths and legends,[*] such positions are real and many departments have staff members who spend their time doing 'admin'. No one knows exactly what they do, as even the simplest of questions about their job will be met with the standard response, 'I'll have to check' and that will be the only response you ever get.[†] More on these admin roles later in the book.

Your Workload will be the biggest point of contention in your working year. Mainly because although it is set at the start of the year, your Head of Department will see no problem in adding new tasks (e.g., an entire extra subject to teach) during the year. Attempts to have any of these new tasks added to your Workload document will be ignored until the end of the year, when you will be thanked for all your efforts and promised that the Workload for the next year will be lighter. But of course it won't.

---

[*] Similar to the ones involving a monster terrorising a small town for no apparently good reason.

[†] This is easily tested. Ask the person in charge of the postgraduate students something obvious, like 'How many postgraduate students do we have?' See, told you they would have to check.

The justification for not reducing it the next year is simple: if you managed to do it this year, then next year it will be even easier as you are now 'experienced'. Surviving the year without having a nervous breakdown is taken as evidence that the Workload was manageable all along.[*]

FAKING A WORKLOAD

All Workloads are a fiction, but fortunately this particular deceit can be made to work both ways. While your Head of Department might generously allocate a full Workload hour for the design and administration of a new subject with 300 students, there are many ways in which you can strike back if you follow these handy tips. Let's start with the easy ones that everyone can do, and move through until we reach the 'Can you really do that?' section.

1. First principles: Check the *theoretical* number/length of lectures (typically, 26 hours) and tutorials (typically, 13 hours) officially listed for your subject. Make sure you insert these numbers in your Workload. Never insert the *actual* numbers of lectures, that is, the lectures and tutorials you couldn't offload after using the following tips.

2. Schedule lectures for Mondays in semester one. There are more public holidays on Mondays than on any oth-

---

[*] I once sat with a Dean who expressed this exact sentiment. The logic they used was essentially this: if you survive (literally survive, as in the 'I survived being attacked by a bear' type of survive) a year of 'excessive teaching', then it clearly wasn't excessive. Therefore, you can do it again next year … and then some.

er day, and far more public holidays in the first semester than the second. Lectures cancelled for holidays are never replaced. You will typically have to move very quickly here as the more experienced staff will swamp the timetable office with requests for Monday classes.[*]

3. Cancel tutorials (part 1). There's no need to have a tutorial in week 1 is there? That can be cancelled easily and rarely arouses suspicion (just say that there are a lot of students enrolling late).

4. Introduce your subject. I have been to a lot of opening lectures that consisted in their entirety of the lecturer talking the students through the *Subject Outline*. No actual subject content whatsoever. This takes care of the week 1 lecture slot. You still have to turn up to the lecture, but you can easily put this one together with no preparation time (a faking of 3–6 'preparation hours' on your Workload).

5. Cancel tutorials (part 2). 'Do you *really* need a tutorial every week?', your Head will ask hopefully as the first week of semester arrives. Momentarily thrown by the multitude of possible intentions behind such a question, coming as it does as in some random brief encounter as you queue behind your Head in the café/at the toilet cubicle, your answer, 'possibly not', is likely to be met with a nodding response that wouldn't look out of place on a toy dog in the back of a car. Basically, your Head wants

---

[*] I recently saw a department where every first year subject was on a Monday. Coincidence? Probably not.

to cut the teaching budget and if you agree to cancel half your tutorials you will be doing them a great favour. Instead of the tutorials in weeks 3, 5, 7, 9, 11 you can give the students some 'self-directed learning'.* If your Head does not initiate this pattern of alternating tutorials, do it anyway (but don't tell your Head). Forgetting to update your Workload to reflect this change is essential.

6. Cancel lectures and tutorials for a whole week (part 1). You can cancel a whole week of teaching, that's one lecture and one tutorial, for 'data collection',† and another if your discipline has an annual conference that has thoughtfully been scheduled during semester time.‡ Given that all the odd-number tutorials have already been cancelled (see point 5 above) hopefully this will be scheduled for an even numbered week.

7. Run an in-class exam. Having a mid-semester exam

---

* This could mean any one of a large range of excellent teaching/learning opportunities, but it doesn't. In reality this means 10 computer-based multiple choice questions (per self-directed week off) all taken from the test bank.

† If your discipline has research students that like to run experiments with undergraduates, you can volunteer your entire class for a week. You will earn kudos points with the research students and your colleagues for being a real team player (good) and you get the week off (very good). Unfortunately attempts to offer more than one week off for data collection will arouse suspicion and should not be attempted. It's still a nice idea though, isn't it?

‡ Once upon a time most universities across the country started and stopped semesters around the same time. Now that there are more terms/semesters than weeks in the year (completely true!) it is now impossible to schedule a conference in a non-teaching period (the only non-teaching period is 25 December to 1 January).

during your regularly scheduled class still counts as two hours of lecturing (plus the preparation time) on your Workload, but all you have to do is sit there while the students fill in a multiple choice test provided by the publisher of your textbook. * If you want to go one step further, put the quiz online and you won't even need to turn up to hand out the exam.

8. Cancel lectures and tutorials for a whole week (part 2). As the in-class exam is going to be tough (if it requires revision, it counts as 'tough') your students will appreciate the time-off to revise. Obviously they won't do any extra revision but you still get the week off. Extra bonuses here are that no students will complain, and your evaluation will probably go up for your thoughtful approach to teaching. Oh, the Irony!

9. Close your subject. Week 13 is the 'Revision lecture'. This can literally be a revision lecture, where you run through some highlights from all the preceding weeks of lectures (all 6–7 of them if you followed the advice above), or an 'open forum' where you tell the students about the exam format (which will probably be multiple choice, see *Examination Meeting*) and answer their probing and insightful questions, reflecting their depth of understanding of the subject materials. As in, 'Will we be asked about *all* the topics we did?', 'Will we have to revise Chapter 7, as that wasn't on the reading lists?', and so on.

---

* It is often fun to have the lecturer(s) and tutor(s) on the subject complete this test as well. See if you can pass your own exam.

10. Remember that two hours on paper is not the same as two hours in the real world. While your lecture is officially 2 hours, no one is going to complain if it finishes early. I recently saw a two-hour lecture conclude after 45 minutes, including 10 minutes of YouTube videos (see below) and 10 minutes of discussion on the forthcoming essay. That year, and for that subject, the lecturer won an award for Teaching Excellence.[*]

11. Get multi-modal. Remember, students don't want to hear you droning on and on: 'Traditional lectures are boring: Use multimedia in your lectures'. Translation, stick a YouTube video-clip into your lecture. Provided it is funny, this can be on any subject, and of any length, even if it is not in any way relevant to the current lecture. The previously sleeping students will all sit bolt upright when the clip starts, each assuming you explained the significance of the clip while they were sleeping.[†]

12. Saving the best for last, you can cancel a lecture and put the video of you giving the lecture from last year (see *Recording Lectures*) online instead.

13. Saving the *even better* for last, cancel *all* the lectures, reclassify your subject as 'Distance education' and put all your lectures from last year online instead.[‡]

---

[*] Completely true.

[†] Added bonus, your *Teaching Evaluations* will be great, students love funny lecturers.

[‡] There are legendary (true) tales of lecturers who arrived to class with a yellowing set of lecture notes that they would – very slowly – proceed to read out to the class. This would go on until about week 3 when the last

Having done all the above, you may well feel that you have successfully cheated the system. However, this is rarely the case as your Head will have anticipated your strategy and already over-filled your Workload. Unsure as to whether the Head has actually read your subject outline, you won't know whether or not to complain as your own lies might get exposed. It's tricky being a lecturer.

---

of the students stopped attending and the lecturer could get back to their research. The modern lecturer can achieve the same basic result by putting their 2005 lecture series online.

4

GETTING READY TO LECTURE

TEACHING QUALIFICATIONS

In the 'good-old-days',[*] the sole qualification for teaching at a university was having a PhD. The assumption was that if you had a PhD that meant you were an expert in your field, and that made you a prime candidate for standing in front of students and imparting that knowledge. Having no charisma and a lecturing style that could induce a catatonic state, were no barrier to a highly successful career. If you were a bad lecturer, this would inspire your students to work that much harder to make sure they kept up. If anything, charismatic and organised lecturers were despised as shallow for making life too easy for the students.[†]

That has all changed. Today a lecturer isn't 'complete' unless they have some form of postgraduate teaching qualification. This completely makes up for the fact that they don't actually know anything about the topics they are teaching. Ask them about the *theory* behind their teaching and they will talk for hours about graduate attributes, learning outcomes and such things. Ask them about the *content* of their teaching and you will hear about whatever it is that the textbook says.

---

[*] Don't you hate people who go on about the good-old-days, and how they were so … good? Well, tough, at university they really were better.

[†] Long ago lecturing was not a popularity contest. It is now.

TEACHING AWARDS

While having a teaching qualification is an essential, it is also *de rigueur* to have won a teaching citation (or several). If you don't have a teaching degree, the titles of some of the award winning teaching going on at your university will be inspirational. Here are some recent winners,[*]

• 'For using problem centred learning pedagogy to achieve high level engagement, enthusiasm and exceptional learning outcomes for diverse students.'

• 'For enabling diverse teacher education cohorts to experience profound engagement in science and sustainability through a blended learning approach.'

• 'For employing peer learning and teaching to successfully support first year students' individual creative development in large class environments.'

• 'For developing a framework to achieve student interaction and a strong student community that lays a foundation for 'soft skills' and motivates students to learn.'

• 'For demonstrating leadership and expertise in the development of design tools and curricula that facilitate the successful embedding of sustainability into undergraduate programs.'

It seems highly likely that there is a website where you can type in a few key words and it will generate the title for a teaching

---

[*] As always, de-identified, but otherwise unchanged. This was all from the website of just one university. Seriously, I couldn't make these up.

award application.[*] If there isn't, there should be.

Reading a list of teaching citations (your university has one just like this) tells you that prizes are to be had for 'enthusing students', 'ensuring flexible student trajectories' and 'stimulating multidisciplinary first year students'.[†]

Whilst some lecturers with teaching citations are in fact really good lecturers, many others are not. However, they are very good at filling in teaching citation applications and this is the important thing.

Why? It's simple, nearly all teaching awards are given out without anyone (other than a few students and what would they know?) actually having *seen* you teach. You could be duller than paint drying-type lecturer, but if you can fill in a form to make yourself sound suitably 'profound', 'diverse' and 'stimulating',[‡] then awards are there for the taking.

Quality teaching is what you say you do, not what you do.

SUBJECT OUTLINES

At the start of the semester you are required to set out the details of your teaching in a Subject Outline (one per subject). This sets out the core details of the subject, the dates and time of lectures, topics to be covered, assessment requirements, and so on.

The 'and so on' comprises:

---

[*] David Bowie used the music industry equivalent to help his songwriting. 'And the shame was on the other side'. Oh yes, it is. Clever guy.

[†] I am not making these up!

[‡] I am so going to start that website for randomly generating teaching award applications.

• A tree wasting[*] cover page with the name of the subject, a university logo and hardly anything else. Note that if the cover features a cartoon this means that the lecturer is going to tell jokes during lectures. Not funny ones, obviously, but at least they are trying to be interesting. If the cover page contains about three different font types, students are advised to check and see if this is really a core subject. That lecturer really doesn't care what anyone thinks of them.

• Another tree wasting page with a copyright declaration. It is worth noting that subject outlines are effectively legal documents. Some universities employ lawyers to take on the role of Dean of Teaching and Learning.[†]

• A page repeating all the details already provided on the cover page, but with a smaller font ('*Timber ...*').

• A page listing your contact details, and that of other staff members who can be contacted if you don't show up to class.[‡]

• A page of warnings telling the students not to steal anyone else's work and pass it off of as their own. This is called plagiarism and it is naughty. Students caught plagiarising can expect to be ... well, nothing really, as they

---

[*] Even though we are in a digital environment, most students still print out the outline

[†] Yes, you read that right. There are so many students complaining about grades, and other subject related issues, that lawyers are needed to check that the outlines will withstand legal challenges.

[‡] Policy is that after a set number of minutes, often 15, an official no-show is declared, so don't ever be late to lectures, especially your own.

are fairly unlikely to be caught if we are honest about it. First, plagiarism software is expensive, or possibly very complicated to install, and a lot of universities don't actually have it.* Needless to say, they try to avoid letting the students know that. Second, have you ever tried using plagiarism software! If a student formats the references in an essay correctly, then that will match with every other student who also writes references correctly. The poor lecturer, seeing a plagiarism score of 35% will initially think the student is a cheat, but when they try deciphering exactly what parts of the essay were 'matches' with other essays, it turns out that there was nothing to be worried about. After doing that wild goose chase a few times, even plagiarism scores of 80% will end up being ignored. No wonder universities don't buy the software.

• A page about student feedback. This is a new addition to outlines. Here, staff have to show that they have taken the feedback from last year's class seriously and duly modified the subject. This includes handling wonderful combinations such as 'do more/do less lectures', and 'have more/have less tutorials', as well as traditional favourites such as 'easier assignments', 'fewer assignments', suggestions to attempt self-reproduction, and so on. The lecturer has to explain how they have changed the subject based on these insightful comments and asking the students to please, please, please provide equally useful feedback this year.

---

* I assume these are reasons for not having the software, although it's possible it is simply not wanted, or maybe Senior Staff believe lecturers can simply 'spot' plagiarism, leap tall buildings in a single bound, that sort of thing.

Basically, your teaching will have to change each year if 1–2 students complain,* the 98–99% who are happy don't actually say 'keep it as it is' so they are outvoted by the noisy minority. What a clever system that is.

• A page about the significance (authority) of the outline. Basically, this says that the outline is fixed and unchangeable, truly an immovable object, but if most of the students want to change something, then OK, change it.

• Several pages of marking rubrics. For each assignment you must provide a detailed breakdown of what the student is required to do to reach a particular grade. For example, submitting your shopping list instead of an essay, will probably result in a Fail.†

It is a little known fact that most lecturers (regardless of what policy may say) will only *increase* a grade after an appeal, operating on the principle: 'students should never be disadvantaged for challenging a grade!' If students actually knew this then they would challenge every single mark, even High Distinctions.‡ The students might also like to know that some staff operate a policy (also unofficial, naturally) of *never* failing a student, barring those who never hand in any assignments (there's no helping some people).

---

* Or express less than total joy in their evaluation comments. See *Student evaluations.*

† Students like you if you give them good grades so never be too harsh, even with shopping lists, especially if they are nicely laid out with few spelling errors.

‡ I have seen students complain even after being given marks in the high 90s, demanding to know *exactly* why each individual mark had been withheld.

The logic here is simple, if you fail a bad student (who has at least tried) then chances are they will come back again next year to try again. This means you will have to read *two* sets of bad assignments. That's too grim a prospect, so just scrape the student a Pass. No-one will mind.

Your outline will have lots of other sections, most of which will require that lawyer to vet them thoroughly before they are unleashed. One (relatively) simple issue is that late penalties, which are applied for each day that an assignment is submitted after the required date. Typically, a set percentage, say 5% of the maximum available marks, are deducted per day. Now does that include weekends? Hardly working days, so should they count? Opinions on that will vary. Smart move here, never put a Friday deadline for an assignment. Always go with a Monday.[*]

Interestingly, many lecturers don't actually apply late penalties. It's rarely worth the effort (the students will hate you) and given that the students who are the worst serial offenders rarely go on to do advanced study, they will soon enough become somebody else's problem.

SPECIAL NEEDS

One other aspect of teaching that bears some consideration is how to handle students with special needs. Your class probably[†] has one or more students with 'special needs' and you will need to adjust your teaching to help get the best out of these students.

----

[*] You can accurately infer the lecturer's rank solely by an analysis of the deadlines for assignments.

[†] Definitely.

That's the theory anyway. What should be an example of lecturers showing that they can adapt and that students can triumph over adversity[*] hits the following stumbling block: no one will tell you that your students have special needs, nor what those needs might be, nor how you could adjust your teaching to reflect those needs.[†]

Somebody really needs to think that policy through.

The closest you will ever get to knowing your students have any special needs is at exam time when you will be told by the examinations office that some (finally named) students will be given extra time to complete the exam. Until that communication, coming as it does at the very end of the teaching period, the lecturer will have had to run the entire subject oblivious to any possibility of helping the students. Despite this, a failure to adapt your teaching to match the special needs of your students will probably result in a poor teaching review in your performance appraisal. A small scream of despair is acceptable at this point in time.

The only other time you will find out a student has special needs is when a complaint is made and the in-house counsellors contact you to make an appointment to discuss the students 'concerns'. In one case I attended such a meeting with a student and two counsellors to address a problem with a grade. We all sat in my office and the student began by saying that they thought my grading had been unfair. I was quite open to that possibility, after all, I'm only human, my marking rubric might have been

---

[*] Both excellent stories, very TV movie of the week.

[†] This ensures they are treated fairly. In this case, that means just like everyone else. This is confusing: do we want to help or not? Guess 'not'.

off,* I might have been distracted while marking, who knows? Error is certainly a possibility in any marking.† I offered my sympathy on these points, and took a look at the essay and found that it had been handed in two weeks late and the mark had been reduced as per the university policy. Thinking we had located the issue, I started to explain the university policy but the student shook his head, as did the counsellors.

No, it wasn't the deduction of late submission marks, the problem was me!

The student explained, and the counsellors nodded along, that it was unfair that I marked his assignments, what with me being an expert in the topic and all that.

Say that again?

His objection, supported by the counsellors, was that a lecturer who was an expert in a topic, couldn't possibly mark his assignment.

I was seriously out of my depth here and called out to two passing colleagues to enter the discussion. One, a Professor patiently explained to the student that it was sort of the point that lecturers were experts, after all, that was how we had got the jobs in the first place and being experts was sort of what we were being paid for, and that this was the thing that made us the ideal people to mark the essays written by students. The student didn't agree, and ended the discussion by running down the corridor kicking bins and tearing down posters.

I think that counts as agreeing to disagree.

---

* A distinct possibility as I didn't have one.
† Even if you have a marking rubric to two decimal places. Who saw that one coming?

There was a happy ending to the story though. Soon after, the student became the President of the Student Union. If you are a fiction writer: go eat your heart out!

MARKING RUBRICS

Students are graded on their work, with most universities operating the following grading codes:

1. Fail
2. Pass
3. Credit
4. Distinction
5. High Distinction

Each of these grades has an associated range of scores (in percentages). For example, in most universities anything under 50% is scored as a Fail; 50–64 is a Pass; 65–74 is a Credit; 75–84 is a Distinction; and anything 85 and over gets a High Distinction.

The micro-details required in a marking rubric would make even a compulsive-obsessive[*] pause and say, 'That's a bit intense'. For each part of an assignment a separate rubric is required. Each with its own micro-grade explanation. For example, a lab report (yes, some disciplines still think scientific reporting is a worthwhile skill to learn) might comprise:

- Title (worth 2% of the grade)
- Abstract (worth 8%)
- Introduction (17%)
- Method (18%)

[*] Or is it 'obsessive-compulsive'? I had better check.

- Results (28%)
- Discussion (22%)
- References (5%)[*]

If the lecturer is lucky, the above will total to 100 (they usually don't – which only gets spotted when marking the things).[†] Within each of these listed parts of the assignment, say the *Title*, a complete breakdown of what kind of answer will result in each of the various grades (Fail through to High Distinction) is needed in the rubric. So too are details of the range of points available within that grade level (getting confused yet?).

For example, the Title in the above example is only worth the full 2%[‡] on offer *if it is perfect*. An ever-so-slightly imperfect title might only be worth 1.9%, which is still a High Distinction (it's equivalent to 95% … of 2%), but obviously not the full 2%.[§] An OK, Credit-ty Title would get between 1.3 (scraped a Credit, or 65% … of 2%) and 1.48 (almost made it to a Distinction, with 74% … of 2%).

Are you confused now? Take a deep breath and read the next sentence very slowly. This … is … how … assignments … get … marked. Each component of an assignment gets its own mi-

---

[*] Some rubrics give marks for spelling and grammar. These are university students and we have to teach them spelling and grammar.

[†] I have seen rubrics that total 115%. Lecturers don't like other lecturers reading their outlines and they really don't like being told that they can't add.

[‡] Quite why it is 2%, and not say 3%, or any other number is *never* considered. If the rubric says it is 2% then that ends all discussion of that topic. All the weightings are essentially arbitrary. Also, who can seriously mark out of 8, 17, 18 or any other random number?

[§] Headaches are commonly reported by staff during marking times. This is why.

cro-mark, and if you want to avoid a withering stare from the Dean of Teaching and Learning, you should add some feedback too. Marking the Title of the assignment could take several minutes, as you try to think of ways to explain why the Title wasn't entirely perfect.

Or you can just slap on an 'Excellent' and give it the full 2%. After all, it's only fair: you wrote the Title when you set the assignment.

Now, a rational person will look at that above scenario and make some very unflattering[*] conclusions about academics, and how the government was right to cut all their funding.

A new academic will look at it and say, 'I really think the title should only be worth 1.5%, the Abstract is worth much more, say 8.5% ...'

An experienced academic will look at it and say … 'I never put the rubrics in my outlines, I give them out (cough, cough)[†] during the semester'.[‡]

A Dean of Teaching and Learning will look at it and see a beautifully designed marking rubric that will prevent all those corrupt lecturers from giving the wrong grades.[§]

Naturally, this last view is the one that prevails.

As with the micro-calculation of Workloads, the essential silliness of trying to work out micro-grades is something that univer-

---

[*] But accurate.

[†] When the Dean of T & L won't be able to see it.

[‡] Such rubrics contain detailed micro-breakdowns like: 'Poor', 'Good', and 'Very good', and not much else. Senior Lecturers don't do rubrics.

[§] Most Teaching and Learning rules are based on the assumption that lecturers give high grades to students they like and bad grades to those they don't like. On this matter, and this matter alone, the Deans of T & L show a remarkable degree of perceptive insight.

sities will not acknowledge.

What's more, the lecturer should be able to offer a convincing argument as to how students *x* and *y*, really do differ, what with their final grades of 64.45 and 64.50 respectively.[*]

By now you should have an idea of how difficult it is to mark an assignment. It is no longer a case of reading it, slapping on a grade and a few 'Well done' sentiments. Each and every part of the assignment has to have a separate micro-mark, and these had better all add up correctly or the students will complain.[†]

To make matters *even more* confusing, some lecturers undergoing what can only be described as a 'brain fart'[‡] impose their own idiosyncratic marking scheme *on top* of each section. For example, I know of one lecturer who personally defines a High Distinction as 80–100%, Distinction as 70–79%, Credit as 60–69; and Pass as 50–60%. To illustrate the resulting problems, a student getting 82% will have been graded at both a Distinction and a High Distinction … at the same time.[§]

Little wonder then that the time for marking assignments has increased significantly. What was once an activity for a lazy Sunday afternoon sprawled on the sofa, is now best conducted at the

---

[*] Final grades are rounded to the nearest whole number, so one of these students will end up with a Pass, the other a Credit. I have sat on many Examination meetings where a staff member will defend their grading to two decimal points. They would argue that these two students really are qualitatively different. They will only retract that statement when it is pointed out that their marking sheet has an error, and the first student actually got 74.45.

[†] It is possible that these micro-marking schemes are an underhand way of teaching students' numerical literacy, in which case they are quite brilliant and I withdraw my complaint.

[‡] Technical term.

[§] As this person is a Head of Department no colleagues will point this out.

computer with the assignment on one side of the screen, and a spreadsheet on the other.[*]

By now you should realise that marking an assignment is a highly complex task, but that is only half of the story. Literally only half of the story.

A MODERATE PROPOSAL

It is now standard practice at universities that grades are 'moderated'. This used to mean that the assignments at the extreme end of the range (the Fails and the High Distinctions) would be double-marked. That is, another lecturer would read these assignments and grade them independently of the first marker. This was always a sensible step and helped to ensure that one marker was not unduly lenient or punitive. Gradually the selection of assignments widened to include a few mid-range offerings (a couple of Passes, Credits and Distinctions).

Unfortunately, the process of evolution in moderating just kept on going: some universities now insist that *all* assignments are double marked.[†] This means that the time required to mark an assignment has effectively halved.

This is because all assignments must be returned within a specified period, usually two, or if you are very lucky three,

---

[*] Throughout this process you must never concede that marking has an element of subjectivity. 'Give me objectivity or give me death', should be your battle cry. It seems to work for the Dean of Teaching and Learning. Quite who would do the dying isn't entirely clear.

[†] It is also common to have 'blind marking' so the students must not put their name on the assignment. Some students take this one step further and sign their emails with their student i.d. number. In an ideal world – according to Deans of T & L – no student would ever identify themselves to a lecturer.

weeks. The first marker must get all their marking done, and then hand over the assignments to another staff member, who will in all probability be even less of an expert in the topic than the first marker.* The second marker then gets on with the double marking. All discrepancies in grades (and – who saw this coming? – there are a lot of those) must be resolved before the assignments are returned. Ever-mindful of the ticking clock (that two-week deadline must be met, or the students will explode), the marking of assignments becomes an all-consuming affair and all other activities suspended for the duration.†

It is difficult to convey the sheer scale and complexity of the work required in the moderation of assignments and it is not uncommon to find staff attending long training courses on the latest moderation practices.‡ While such efforts are driven by noble motives§ it does then seem odd that most teaching is done by graduate students who are being paid by the hour to deliver lectures that they didn't write and run tutorials they don't understand. There is a major disconnect here between all the efforts to ensure teaching quality in theory, and what happens in practice.

Happily, there is a brilliant solution: make your assessments multiple choice. When there is a single 'right answer' then there

---

* In that they won't have any knowledge of the topic, or possibly even the entire discipline area.

† Eating. Sleeping. Seeing your family. Nothing important.

‡ I have recently sat through a 92 slide presentation on moderation principles. The person presenting was a T & L expert, but didn't know how to use fly-ins so each bullet point was a new slide. I know this because they gave us all 92-page colour handouts of the presentation. Printed one slide to a page of course.

§ I hope they are. It is very easy to make a case that they are the product of pure evil.

is nothing very much to moderate.*

BUT WAIT, THERE'S MORE

In addition to explaining how your marking rubric works lecturers are also required to detail how the subject, and each piece of assessment, contributes to the generic skills a student will learn (graduate attributes), the subject specific learning outcomes, and the course learning outcomes. All this information should be included in your outline, which by now should be around about 15–18 pages long (assuming you use a very small font).

Compiling the outline, having it proofed and debugged (if you are lucky someone might spot the marks don't add up) will take several working days,† but it's all worth it in the cause of improved higher education standards.

Except of course, the students won't read it. They never do.

MENTAL ARITHMETIC

It would be fair to say that the above processes have resulted in many lecturers completely losing touch with any semblance of reality. This can be illustrated with the following real-life, actual, as really done by students, exam paper. The exam had a set time of 2 hours plus 10 minutes reading time. The exam was worth 50% of

---

* Not always true. I had one student who disagreed with the 'correct' answers on a multiple choice exam and when given a copy of the answer sheet, came back a day later with detailed rebuttals for all their 'incorrect' answers, showing that in each case their answer *could have been correct* … if it was a Wednesday, in Melbourne, and it was raining. Lesson here – never give out the answer sheet.

† Rarely ever allowed for in Workload calculations.

the overall grade for the subject. The opening instructions were:

> Answer ALL questions in Section A (6 marks) and Section B (54 marks), and answer ONE question in SECTION C (25 marks). Total of 85 marks.

A total of 85 marks? Why not 100? To give an overall percentage mark for the exam you would have to add an extra layer of calculation, dividing the number of marks given by 85, then multiplying by 100 to give the percentage score. Oh well, no big deal I suppose.

Pressing on, we can take a look at how the marks are allocated in each of the three exam sections (A, B & C).

> SECTION A (6 marks)
> The value of each question is 1 mark.
>
> SECTION B (54 marks)
> 1. 5 marks
> 2. 3 marks
> 3. 5 marks
> 4. Part a. 5 marks
>   Part b. 5 marks
> 5. 5 marks
> 6. 6 marks
> 7. 5 marks
> 8. Part a. 5 marks
>   Part b. 5 marks
>   Part c. 5 marks
>
> SECTION C (25 marks)
> The value of the question is 25 marks.

Remember, the students had 10 minutes reading time for this exam. The Secret Lecturer hopes that they were allowed to bring a calculator (or possibly a spreadsheet program) so they could answer the following Secret Lecturer Questions (SLQs):

SLQ1: If the exam is marked out of 85, and the exam is worth 50% of the overall subject mark, how much is each individual mark in the exam worth to the subject? (Worth 1 mark.)*

SLQ2: How much time should be allocated to completing sections A, B and C respectively? (Worth 3 marks, one per section.)†

SLQ3: How long should be allocated to completing each of the questions in section 2? (Worth 11 marks, one mark each for questions 1, 2, 3, 5, 6 & 7; two marks for question 4; and three marks for question 8.)‡

SLQ4: True or false. The lecturer who wrote this exam won a Teaching Award for this subject for this year? (Worth 47.506 marks.)§

---

* SLQ1: Easy. If an exam that is worth 50% of the subject, has 85 marks, then each exam mark (50/85) is worth an easy-to-remember 0.588 of the overall mark for the subject. What could be simpler?

† SLQ2: Also easy. There are 85 marks and the exam is 120 minutes long, therefore $85/120 = 0.708$ minutes per mark. Hang on, or is it $120/85 = 1.412$? I wish I had paid more attention in maths class at school. You then multiply one of those numbers by 6 (section A), 54 (Section B) and then 25 (Section C). Add up those three numbers and if it equals 120(ish) you used the right number, if not, do it again substituting the other number. I think ...

‡ SLQ3: Calm. Calm. Taking from SLQ2, we multiply 0.708 (or possibly 1.412) x the number of marks per question and then convert that decimal number into minutes. We do that for each question and each sub-question, that's, let me check, 11 separate calculations. Neat. Now, how long do I have left to read the questions before I get started writing answers? What do you mean the exam ended an hour ago?

§ SLQ4: I won't tell you the answer, but here's a clue: if I did it would make you cry.

STUDENT EVALUATIONS

As the semester (or teaching period) nears its end, students are asked[*] to provide feedback on the subject through a student satisfaction survey. This is done anonymously, so every student you have offended in some way now has a chance for revenge. Not only will they take it, but they will get their friends to join in too. However, the flipside is also true. Every student you have 'wowed' will also submit feedback, and they too will get their friends to join in too. The ones in the middle of all that hate and love, don't do anything. Your evaluation for your teaching centres on the ratio of revenge to adoration amongst your students. In a world of 'averages', oddly enough there are no 'average students' completing evaluations. Funny that.

Student evaluations are typically done in a multiple-choice format, essentially asking students to respond to questions such as:

- I found this subject intellectually stimulating

- The subject was well organised

- The subject helped me to develop skills and knowledge

- The methods of assessing student work were fair and appropriate

- I received feedback that assisted my learning

Amazingly, the answers to these questions are the ones that will officially determine whether or not you are a good or bad lecturer. The five available response options are:

---

[*] Asked. Cajoled. Solicited. Begged. Bribed. Failing to get a high enough response rate is going to result in a telling off from the Dean of T & L.

- Strongly disagree
- Disagree
- Neutral
- Agree
- Strongly agree

Even though there are five main questions, the answers to each question are averaged, then rounded, and then averaged again,[*] this is so that your entire evaluation can be reduced to a single (whole) number.

All that your Dean of Teaching and Learning cares about is that final number. If the percentage saying 'Agree/Strongly agree' is above the set 'threshold for quality teaching', which is, say 70%,[†] then you have had a good semester. Fall below that threshold, say 69%, and you have some *serious* explaining to do. Curiously the students who failed to agree or strongly agree that, 'The subject helped me to develop skills and knowledge' etc., are all lumped together as a dissatisfied mass. Students who really hated you are lumped in with those who thought you were a bit '*meh*'.[‡]

It should be noted here that there is no attempt to *really* benchmark or standardise any of these results. That would result in a normal distribution (See *A normal distribution*) of evaluations and that would mean a *range* of responses. Some of these would be … below average! Instead, in theory, every university can happily report that all their subjects receive 'excellent teach-

---

[*] I think I might have missed another rounding at the end, but it's simply not worth getting too fussed about the details here.

[†] Why 70? This seems to be an arbitrary number, but once it is set, it *really* matters.

[‡] Cool young person's slang. Try using it in your lectures. Unless it is now dated, in which case, don't.

ing evaluations'.* Happily, that is exactly what happens in practice. Teaching standards these days are very, very high.

In addition to this numerical fun, student evaluations also incorporate open text, or qualitative feedback. This fleshes out the love-hate ratings very nicely, as the feedback is either so good it will make you blush, or so bad it will have you rethinking your career path.

I was lucky enough to have a Dean who took such comments very, very seriously, so much so that if a staff member had a good numerical score, but one student said something mildly 'constructive', then the teaching on that subject would need to be radically overhauled next year. A truly knee-jerk reaction. So why was I fortunate to have such a Dean? Well, the university in its wisdom thought that the staff should provide ratings of the Dean, using a similar set of metrics and open-text boxes. You could tell the evaluation had gone badly because the day before the results were released the Vice-Chancellor sent round a long memo telling staff to (a) not be so mean, and (b) that qualitative feedback is a 'guide' and that it shouldn't be taken too seriously. Needless to say, the Dean's evaluations were horrific. Sometimes the system works.†

BAD GRADES

At the moment the teaching evaluation system is like the *Sword of Damocles*, hanging over the heads of staff. The message is clear:

---

* Very Lake Wobegon: All the lecturers are above average. Oh look it up!
† But not as well as it should: No-one overhauled the Dean for the next year.

make your students happy, or else. Lecturers, occasionally being smart types who read research reports, or at least spend too long taking to burnt-out Associate Professors, believe that the number-one predictor of student evaluations is … can you guess … grades. Students with good grades give good evaluations; students with bad grades give bad evaluations.

The solution is simple: avoid giving bad grades.

Unfortunately, as clever as that idea is, it isn't going to work.[*] Even if you could give every student a High Distinction, some would still complain, so we have to be a little more careful with our solutions. For a start, not all students expect to get top grades and many are happy just to Pass.[†] Others will see a Credit or Distinction as a great success. These are normal, real students. They do exist.

The trick in *grading for evaluative success*[‡] is therefore to give each student a 'happy mark',[§] relative to their expectations! As such, the solution to grading for evaluative success isn't to 'avoid giving bad grades', it should read 'avoid giving bad grades to the wrong students'. That removes most of the hatred from the student body. To instil some love, you should then make sure that the good grades are given to those who either demand it, or those who will be the happiest to get such nice news. Being a lecturer is a lot like being Santa Claus: all the joy you get to spread is wonderful.

---

[*] And things seemed to be going so well.

[†] I have encountered students who on hearing that they scored 51% on a subject asked 'Where did I go wrong?' They were aiming for 50% and getting 51% meant that they had done more work than they needed to. No, they were not joking.

[‡] I think I have just invented a cliché. Cool.

[§] Literally, one that will make them happy.

Finally, it is worth commenting on sample sizes. Most universities work on the principle that there should be a minimum number of responses for an evaluation to be meaningful.

That number is 'one'.

If at least one student completes an evaluation, then the lecturer's work in that subject can be reviewed. If the one student liked you, then your 100% satisfaction rating will see your subject listed at the top of the faculty rankings. However, if the student did not like you (hatred or indifference are the same thing here), then you will be at the bottom of the faculty rankings.[*]

---

[*] Either way, your Head of Department and/or your Dean will show an understanding of basic statistics that a six-year-old would recognise as a 'bit dodgy'.

5

THE LOST ART OF LECTURING (REDISCOVERED)

LECTURES

Assuming you have made a right mess of your Workload (i.e., failing to fake it), you will be required to 'do' some lectures.

It is popularly believed that lecturers are experts in the subjects they teach, but as already detailed in this book, that is rarely, if ever, the case. Instead, the average lecturer[*] will often know as much about the subject they are teaching, as say, the students they are teaching.

However, this is rarely a problem. Some facts will relieve any stress and anxiety you might feel about giving a two-hour lecture on a topic you know nothing about.

1. The students will not have read the textbook. This only gets read prior to assignments, and even then, only the parts that will be assessed. Assume the students know nothing, and you will rarely be wrong.[†]

---

[*] I've already done that line, twice.
[†] All except the intense one who never misses lectures, sits at the front of the class and seems to be taking note of everything you say.

2. Students never ask questions. If any students do turn up to your lectures, once again, don't be scared, they are probably just lost, or looking for a nice place to sleep.* No one will ask you any questions that will expose your lack of knowledge. If you do ever get a real question, shortly after the Angels stop singing, say this: 'That is a very good question, very interesting, and I'll come back to that in a later part of the subject'. They won't remember.

3. Be a 'smart' lecturer. While many lecturers rely on the PowerPoint slides produced by the textbook publishers, you can amaze your students with your depth of academic knowledge, by using the slides prepared by the publisher of *another* textbook. To your students these slides will seem vaguely familiar (If they have glanced at the sub-headings in the set textbook) but fresh enough to make it *look like*[†] you really know the subject.

Writing lectures is clearly not nearly as complicated as it is made out to be. In fact, many lecturers rely on the slides provided by the textbook publisher. In theory, the idea here is that you add to the content of the provided slides in your narration,[‡] perhaps illustrating certain points with material from the textbook, or your own background reading.[§] However, the way this works in practice differs slightly from that, and is basically as follows.

---

* I once worked at a university near a very nice surfing beach. In Winter students would turn up to class in wetsuits and proceed to fall asleep at the back of the lecture theatre where it was nice and warm.

† Perception is everything.

‡ You know, the bit of the lecture where you talk.

§ Just kidding.

Suppose you have a slide which contains the following hypo-thetical text:

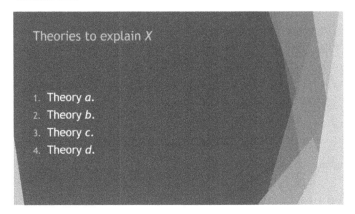

First, note the generic PowerPoint background template.[*] Also note the heading in a different colour, denoting it is a heading (very clever that), and the fairly generously sized font used in the main body of the slide. All in all, a bland, but essentially effective slide. A bit short on content, but you can hardly put an entire lecture in a PowerPoint slide, can you?[†]

Now, how do you present this slide in a lecture?

Remember our assumption is that you know nothing about the subject: you have probably not even read the textbook.[‡] With

---

* Your university will have a PowerPoint template for lectures. No one uses it.

† Did you just hear the silence in response to that question? Of course you can put an entire lecture on a PowerPoint slide. Just drop the font size to something unreadable at further than 20 centimetres from the screen and it can be done.

‡ You meant to, but didn't get the time, what with all the teaching you have to do.

those assumptions in place, here is the Secret Lecturer's guide to how to lecture using the example slide. The complete (not a word missing) narration you provide while this slide is displayed is as follows:

> There are at least[*] four theories of X.
> First, we have theory a.
> Second, we have theory b.
> Third we have theory c.
> *And finally*, we have theory d.

See, wasn't that easy? The secret to lecturing is ... (drum roll please) ... you read out the slides!

The super-secret is ... (where's that drum roll?) ... you paraphrase ... occasionally!

Obviously, don't paraphrase too much or you might get lost and say something that is ... (melodramatic sound effects please) ... original![†]

Please feel free to adapt the above delivery system as necessary for your own lectures. Make it reflect your own personality. In the above example our lecturer changed their intonation pattern ('*And finally*') and really brought the entire slide to life. *You* could emphasis *theory c*. The choice is yours.

Use this handy lecturing guide and next time you are asked to cover an entire subject, 'but we will provide the slides', you can accept, safe in the knowledge that you could deliver it like a seasoned professional. A teaching citation is practically guaranteed.

---

[*] Always adopt a cautious approach to stating facts. Especially when you don't have any.

[†] At least one student will ask: 'Will this be on the exam?'

RECORDING LECTURES

Many universities insist that all lectures are recorded, so that the modern students can study in a way that fits their 'style of learning'.* The only downside to this brilliant innovation is that lecturers will often find themselves giving a lecture to room with just a handful of really keen-types and a few sleeping surfers.

However, on the plus side, if you do record your lectures, the recordings can be made available to students in the following years, meaning that you don't have to attend your own lecture![†] One tip here is to avoid mentioning any dates or topical events in your lectures. It is a complete give-away if your lecture recording opens with a reference to the 'terrible events in New York last week'.

TUTORIALS

Tutorials were once the highlight of a students' time at university. A chance to sit one-on-one with a staff member, to vigorously debate some grand theoretical problem, or in the very best universities, an opportunity to drink lots of beer while your lecturer wrote notes on the back of a beermat.[‡] Today, tutorials are more like mini-lectures, with about 25 students per class. There's no way 25 people can have a discussion where everyone participates: assuming the tutor says nothing, each student could only talk for an average of two minutes.

---

* Note that you must bend to their will, not the other way round. We are *so* preparing them for the real world.

† You have to admire lecturers who actually do this.

‡ My PhD was designed on the back of a beermat (YR). My supervisor was a contributor to a leading good beer guide and most supervision sessions were conducted off-campus … in pubs.

But that idealised scenario is never going to happen. Apart from the problem of you having to constantly explain things (about half the tutorial), there will always be a handful of students who like the sound of their own voices (shame really as they are never the bright ones), and far more who will say nothing (shame really, as they often *are* the bright ones).

The actual number of students in a tutorial is an interesting example of how the bending of space and time is possible.[*] The starting premise is simple, tutorials should be small groups, say 8–10 students, but everyone knows that most students don't come to class and the actual number of attendees will probably only be 3–4. Consequently, allocating a much larger number, say 20–25, as the theoretical class size isn't too much of a stretch, since only 8–10 will actually attend. All good so far.

Now, just in case *all* the students should all suddenly decide to come to class[†] a big room will need to be booked, one that could hold all 25 students.

Now, having booked such a big room, and knowing that most students don't come to class, it is entirely logical to allocate about 35–40 students to that class.

By now I think you can see where this is going. In short, tutorials with 25 plus students have become standard practice. Rather than try to get them all talking, it is far easier for the person running the tutorial to do most of the talking, and so the session becomes a mini-lecture (minus any reasonable preparation time).

---

[*] See Einstein's *Special Theory of Tutorials*.

[†] A sure sign of the impending Apocalypse, clearly listed in the *Book of Revelations* (The University Lecturer's Edition).

STUDENT RETENTION

Once a student has enrolled in your class they should not under any circumstances, be allowed to withdraw. There are no exceptions to this rule. If one of your students drops out, then your retention rate drops and that will mean that you are a bad lecturer. This must not happen.

One way to keep students happy is to provide early feedback. This will probably be a directive from your Dean of Teaching and Learning. One way to give early feedback is to run, in week 2 or 3, a multiple-choice test, worth about 5% of the overall grade. This can be scored instantly and the resulting feedback will either tell the students that they really should revise for tests (good outcome), or more probably that the subject is way harder than they thought it would be and so they should withdraw (bad outcome).

Long ago this process of culling the weaker students would have been seen as all very fine and sensible, just the sort of thing that universities should do. Now, it is seen as evidence that the lecturer is doing a bad job and in need of a swift rebuke from their Head of Department.

This awful scenario can be avoided entirely if the test only provides positive feedback. This is easily arranged by making the multiple-choice questions so mind-numbingly easy that it would require some effort NOT to score a perfect 10.[*] The resulting student feedback, in all cases 'You are doing very, very well', will result in all the students thinking that the subject is easy and that

---

[*] Here's how to make sure all students get high grades: (1) Practice all the questions in a tutorial; (2) When you list each question mark the correct one in bold and with an '*' (3) Only have one answer.

they are on track for a High Distinction overall.[*] As a result, they will stay in the subject, little realising that the later assessments are going to be set by a psychopath intent on achieving a 'normal distribution of marks' (see *A normal distribution*).

There are many ways in which a student can fail a subject and so there are usually multiple ways to record the reasons for that fail. For example, the student who never came to class and didn't submit any assignments might be given – no one knows why – the Code NN.[†] While there are many sub-classifications for Fail grades (e.g., NW, NX, NC, NS, & NN as different types of Fail grade), there is only one underlying cause of failure: you! If a student even fails to attend your subject, that too is your fault.[‡]

A NORMAL DISTRIBUTION

As if marking wasn't already complicated enough (see *Marking rubrics*), your university will have a policy that grades for a subject should be 'normally distributed'.

Over time, and with a large sample of marks, clear patterns

---

[*] Note that hard assessments with large weightings should not be scheduled early in semester.

[†] The actual letter codes vary from university to university, but are all equally counter-intuitive. Academic staff are not normally told about the variety of fail grades until they attend an *Examination Meeting*, when the new list ('valid as of 11pm yesterday') will be produced by the Dean of T& L who will berate all attending staff for failing to keep up with important university rules.

[‡] This can easily be remedied by having you make a phone call to each and every student to ask them if they are OK, if there's anything you can do for them, and so on. No, I am not kidding. This is standard practice in some universities where even the Year 12 students who expressed an interest in attending the university, but never got round to enrolling, can expect a personal call from a member of the lecturing staff.

in the distribution of grades are evident, and your university will suggest that say, there should be 5% of students getting a High Distinction, 15% a Distinction and so on.

This is all perfectly sensible and fine, until it is applied to every single subject (see *Examination Meeting)* and taken as a target that *has to be met.* Your Dean of Teaching and Learning will look at the grade distribution for your subject, tut-tut very loudly, and announce that you have failed to achieve a normal distribution. You must have been too lenient/too punitive,[*] which is exactly what all those damned rubrics and moderation processes were trying to prevent. Are you some kind of idiot? Do you not understand university policy?

And so on.

While there is a small grain of sense in the idea of normal distributions, this takes a very long walk of a short pier when applied to a class of say 10 students. Typical conversations will go something like this:

> Dean of T & L: Only 5% of students are supposed to get High Distinctions, you have 10%.
> Lecturer: That was one student. One student represents 10% of the total.
> Dean of T & L: I understand that[†]. But your distribution is off. Try to have a better marking rubric next year, something that discriminates more accurately.
> Lecturer: Or, perhaps I could cut my students in half?

---

[*] The possibility that every now and then that you might have a slightly higher than average number of either very good or very bad students is an idea that is best kept to yourself.

[†] No they don't.

Dean of T & L: I don't want to interfere in how you do your job,[*] so I leave that up to you.

While most universities stick rigidly to their expected distribution patterns, some are engaging in a form of academic arms race to see who can give the most 'high grades'.[†] In some universities the percentage of students being awarded the highest grades (Distinction and High Distinction) has increased each year, such that around – wait for this – 90% of students graduate with one of the top two grades. This fact[‡] then becomes part of a marketing ploy to encourage new recruits. Officially, all universities offer 'excellent' teaching', so this grading information becomes the key point of differentiation. Given the choice between going to a university where 25% of students get the highest two grades, versus another that offers a 90% rate, as a student, which would you choose?

In most cases disputes about whether a distribution is acceptable centre on the higher end marks, such as how many High Distinctions have been given. However, there are also equally heated debates about the percentage of Fail grades. As noted earlier, if a student fails, it is always the fault of the lecturer, so if a large number of students fail, then the lecturer has a really big problem. Australian universities have a very dark secret that occasionally

---

[*] Yes, they do. Also, Deans of T & L don't get sarcasm, or other any other forms of humour for that matter.

[†] The grading system should be changed to reflect reality. There are only three real grades: High Distinction, Distinction, and Who Cares?

[‡] It is a *fact* in that this is happening (year-on-year, a higher percentage of students are being given higher grades), but it is hard to believe as *fact* the idea that every year for the last decade or so students have become objectively smarter than the students in the preceding years.

breaks surface, and it is this: certain degrees have large numbers of overseas students and failing those students, is not an option.

My own experience of this situation is sadly not that unique a story. I once had to teach a subject where nearly all of the students (around 60) were from overseas. The first assessment was an extended essay, and these were generally excellent, with large numbers of students handing in extremely high quality work. Then came the written exam. The exam scripts were in most cases, blank, or consisted of a couple of scribbled lines in broken English. Students who had scored 45/50 in the first assessment received grades of 0/50 in the exam, leaving them with an overall Fail grade. Over half of the students in the class had submitted almost flawless essays, but under exam conditions, could not write a single sentence in English. I gave an overall Fail grade to most of the class.

A few days after submitting my final results I was urgently summoned to meet my Head of Department, who began by telling me what a bad lecturer I was, and how my grading was overly punitive and so on. In reply I pulled out some of the worst exam scripts and asked how anything other than a zero was appropriate?

Silence.

I offered a theory, that the students had either 'bought' or plagiarised their essays. I could see no other explanation for the extreme variations in the assessment items.

After some more silence I was told that the university had long suspected that in some programs that the overseas students were buying assignments. My subject seemed to offer proof that this fraud was real. I was told that action would be taken to remedy the problem.

The remedy was as follows: my final results were amended ('moderated') by someone (I have no idea who) and I later found out that all 60 students had passed. I was also removed from teaching that subject again.

6

THE DARK ARTS OF RESEARCH

GETTING INTO RESEARCH

As an undergraduate student I once came across a research paper comparing the experiences of children in two-day care centres, one in a run-down neighbourhood[*] in London, and the other in the Bahamas. The researchers (there were a lot of them) had spent a couple of months in each location conducting fieldwork. Their conclusion seemed to be that the day care centre in the Bahamas was very nice, and they were planning to go there again for a follow-up study.

It was at that point that I knew I wanted to be a researcher.

Subsequent experience reinforced this desire. At my first post-graduate university[†] the astro-physics department (do we still have any of those?) were always off doing fieldwork in Hawaii, where there is a very good telescope high up on a mountain. As it was only used at night (who knew?), the researchers spent their days on the beach.

Now some will say that researchers are driven to solve problems, the answers to the big questions of 'life, the universe and

---

[*] Where their researchers' university was located.

[†] Showing off. I have lots of degree certificates in very nice frames. They live in a cardboard box in my garage.

everything'. But in most cases its much baser reasons, say 'fame, fortune and everything that goes with it'. My own aim is for sun-drenched beaches, I'm not there yet, but I'm not going to stop trying.[*]

Here's how you might get your own research career on track. A word of advice, it's not worth spending too long on this idea as it's not as if anyone hired you for your research ability. That PhD wasn't the reason you got the job: that teaching certificate though, that's quite another story.

PUBLICATIONS

I like writing articles for publication. I am lucky that I can write academic pieces pretty well[†] and I do interesting (sometimes cutting-edge) research that is genuinely original and exciting.

Well, that's what I tell myself. The reviewers seem to have quite a different idea.

I have a list[‡] of journal editors that I will never ever speak to again (short of a zombie apocalypse) and a list of supposedly anonymous reviewers that I can instantly recognise by their writing styles.[§] Getting articles accepted for publications is hard, with many journals openly bragging about their 90% (or more) rejection rate.

---

[*] A very successful colleague of mine had the following saying pinned to his door: 'Even Professors need a Porsche'. His was red. It went very fast. He was a real inspiration to his students … and colleagues.

[†] The current book may be used as evidence to refute that point if you wish.

[‡] It's quite a long list.

[§] Try to avoid using infrequently used words and expressions, frequently. It is like signing your name!

An example. A few days ago I submitted and article and got it back, rejected, after all of 45 minutes. The editor admitted he hadn't read it, had only skimmed the abstract, but the title told him all he needed to know: a study with a sample of two could not possibly be interesting.*

In order to engage in this ritual of humiliation, you need to have a really thick skin. It also helps if you are the editor of a journal and can 'do swaps' with the editor of the journal you want to publish in. The rule here is: you take one of mine, I'll take one of yours. In some disciplines this practice is so out of control papers are submitted, reviewed and accepted inside an hour. The swaps continue and each author agrees to cite the papers of the other, very quickly producing citation classics that only two people have ever read.†

Given this rampant corruption, many have questioned why do we bother?

The answer is simple: having lots of publications on your CV is essential to convincing your university NOT to give you even more teaching to do. If you can convince the university that you are 'research active'‡ then they will not attempt to redefine your Workload. That 40% research component on your Workload is sacred, and if that goes then the amount of teaching you will be doing in the next year will make you look like a Teaching Fellow on steroids.

---

* Ever-so politely I pointed out that the 'two' the editor had seen in the abstract referred to *two countries* and much to my surprise I was asked to resubmit the paper. I didn't bother, I sent it somewhere else where they will hopefully read it before rejecting it.

† Given the speed of acceptance, the word 'read' is probably not appropriate. Substitute: 'looked at' and you get slightly closer to the truth.

‡ What a wonderful expression.

So here is something of a puzzler, you need to publish, but can't. What to do? Luckily the Secret Lecturer can help with this quick guide to faking the publication list on your CV.

1. The first rule is that quantity matters. Sure, some will talk about having one paper with massive *impact*,[*] but that idea is practically prehistoric. Length of publication list is everything. More publications = happy Head of Department = happy lecturer. Got that clear, let's get going with the faking.

2. What is a publication anyway? You may hear talk of A1s, C1s, C2s and so on.[†] No need to bother yourself with any of that silliness. When faking it you throw all your publications into the mix.

Got no publications? Don't make me laugh, of course you do. How about that subject outline you just wrote? That counts as a publication.[‡] I know of a university where the student essays on a Subject are compiled into a journal format and these essays are recorded as departmental publications. Tragically the lecturer never thinks to claim supervisory privileges and doesn't put their name on each essay as co-author. Shame, they would have a really great CV.

Rule here, if you write something, then it might be as

---

[*] This means exactly the opposite of whatever you think it means.

[†] If you don't recognise that, I hope you really like teaching because you are going to do a lot of it.

[‡] Some will scoff at this advice. In response I will show them that I have a subject outline on my *h-index*! Who's laughing now?

well be listed as a publication. I have also seen this principle applied to the university website entry of a lecturer[*] (utterly brilliant!) and each entry on a blog (that's how to get a really long publication list). Putting Twitter postings is probably overdoing it though. If the citation is longer than the original content, you probably don't want to draw attention to that fact.

3. Conference papers are publications (part 1). You can list all your conference papers in your publications list, provided you bury them in the middle of some real publications. Sure, they don't *really* count but we are going for volume: dazzle the reader with a CV that gets onto multiple pages. When you put the details of the presentation, if you format it really badly (leave out dates, venue, and of course, the words 'conference' and 'paper', etc.) it might even look like a real publication. That is, provided the person reading it doesn't look too closely.

4. Conference papers are publications (part 2). If you are very lucky (or very smart), you will try to go to conferences that publish the abstracts of papers as an online appendix to a journal. This counts as a publication![†] Note that if the journal is a good one[‡] your ResearchGate[§] index will jump nicely. Five 'impact points' for a 150-word

---

[*] Yes, they put their staff profile in their CV as if it was a publication.

[†] Actually it is not, but ignore that minor technicality.

[‡] We really don't need to get into that do we? They are all good for faking purposes.

[§] Every academic has an account with *ResearchGate* (or *Academia.edu)*, except for those that don't.

abstract? Thank you very much.[*]

5. Write 'replies' to published articles. Some journals are happy to print almost anything to show that someone has actually read one of their articles, so a quick reply, or a letter to the editor will do you nicely as another publication. Note, the trick here is to give your letter/reply an exciting title,[†] make it sound like it is an original article.

6. Pay for it (part 1). If you have a manuscript laying around doing nothing, say your PhD thesis, there are plenty of publishers who will happily publish it, for a fee. The only person who will buy it will be you, but it now means you can split your CV into 'Books' and 'Other publications', just like a real lecturer![‡]

7. Pay for it (part 2). There are also plenty of 'predatory' journals who will happily publish *anything*. Literally, anything. My favourite such article is the 2014 masterpiece by Mazières and Kohler entitled 'Get me off your f___ing mailing list'.[§] These seven magical words, repeated hundreds of times over ten pages (with two quite brilliant figures) was published, all for the bargain price of $150.

---

[*] This is such an easy fake that I know some postgraduate students with no 'real' publications who have higher ResearchGate scores than their Professors. Please don't take these online sites too seriously.

[†] If you call it 'Letter to the editor' or 'A reply to …' and put that on your CV it will look like a fake publication. A fake that looks fake? Can't have that.

[‡] Also note that you can actually buy ISBN numbers (there are discounts for bulk purchases), so you can make even shopping lists sound like real books.

[§] Quite real. Look it up.

Basically, a predatory journal will run a fake peer review (the above article was forced to make some *very* profound changes) and accept the article ... as soon as your credit card details have gone through.

While predatory journals are an awful thing, having a few bogus papers buried in your CV will add bulk, which is the important thing. Paying for a few predatory publications is possibly a good financial transaction, especially if your university puts money in your research account for every paper you publish.

Now you are probably thinking (always a good thing) that the Secret Lecturer has *jumped the shark*,[*] no modern university would fall for such nonsense. Well nonsense to that, they sure do.

I like reading staff publication profiles[†] and at one university in one department I know there are several staff members with publication lists that are straight out of the Secret Lecturer's playbook.[‡] If you were to delete all the above fakery, several page CVs would shrink to something you could easily squeeze into a footnote. To make matters even more surreal, some of those staff were recently promoted and are now in charge of telling other staff how to do their research.

The cycle of fakery goes on.

---

[*] No idea? Get out a bit more.

[†] No idea why, I just do.

[‡] Actually, that isn't surprising as I based the guide on those pages, but that's not important right now.

7

ADMINISTRATION

MORE ADMINISTRATORS THAN LECTURERS

In the modern university there are more admin staff than academic staff.[*] I recently received an updated list of the admin staff in my College[†] which organised the admin staff into 23 different groupings. That's not 23 different admin staff members, that's 23 different admin *sections*, each with multiple staff, and that's just for my College.

There are so many admin staff in your university that it would cost less to remove all those staff and to give every lecturer their own full-time personal assistant. Even more money could be saved if those same people could be persuaded to cut the grass.

Sadly, that idea has yet to catch on. That's a shame really, as no one can explain exactly what it is that all the admin staff actually do. Nearly every task that you would think the admin staff would do, is actually done by the academic staff.

Remember, all staff are given 20% of their Workload for ad-

---

[*] Quite true.

[†] College (*defin.*): A arbitrary cluster of academic disciplines that will be described as a coherent grouping, or will be until the next university restructure when an entirely different cluster will become an even more coherent grouping. Even though it was the same as the one from two restructures ago …

min purposes.

If you take that fact in isolation, it is curious to realise how academics willingly sign up for a job where *20% of their time* (minimum) is given over to admin. Bet no-one thought about that when they decided to become a lecturer.

ACADEMIC PROCEDURES: HIRING CASUALS

One of the constants of modern universities is an obsession, bordering on the pathological, with 'procedures'. Everything has to be done following correct procedures, but as these change from year to year (sometimes more frequently) staff are often caught out by trying to use the 'old procedures'. For example, at one university I visit frequently, the process for hiring a casual employee goes something like this:

1. Lecturer requests written permission of their Head to employ a casual. After much shuffling of Workload papers approval is granted.

2. Lecturer identifies potential casual and asks if they would like to be considered for a position at the university.

3. Lecturer seeks permission from College Manager[*] to hire the named casual.

4. College Manager seeks permission from the Dean to hire the casual.

---

[*] No one is really sure what a College Manager does, nor how they got the job in the first place (they appear from one day to next without any warning). Despite this, they are powerful and can make your life hell. The latter is probably part of their job description.

5. College admin staff ask lecturer to complete part 1 of contract offer form for casual.

6. College sends contract form to casual to complete part 2 and sign.

7. Casual returns completed and signed contract.

8. Contract goes to College Manger for signing.

9. Contract goes to Dean for signing.

10. Casual is sent letter of offer of position.

11. Unopened letter of offer of position returned to university; potential casual has been offered full-time position at another university and moved city.

12. Head tells lecturer that there is no longer any budget for casuals and that they will have to do the required teaching.

Clearly, the above procedure did not spring fully-formed from the university's policy database. Instead, it is an evolutionary process, but in reverse. Basically, if an adaptation (in this case a change in procedure) is deemed beneficial, then it is jettisoned. If an adaptation is pointless and time-consuming then it is maintained.

One important lesson for lecturing staff is that if you are trying to employ a casual, make sure that person has no skills or talents that would in any way make them attractive to another employer.

ACADEMIC PROCEDURES: PURCHASING EQUIPMENT

The procedures for purchasing equipment (e.g., lab equipment, computers) are equally complex, but with even greater potential for delays. For example, I once ordered a computer and after all the necessary paperwork, and several months delay* I received an email from the supply office telling me that the computer had arrived. Overjoyed, I ran down the stairs to the building where the supply office was located. Except it wasn't.

Checking I was going to the place specified in the email, I walked the corridors looking for the entrance to the supply office. There was no such room number. About to give up, I noticed a door at the end of an unlit corridor and went to investigate. A small sign on the door said that this was indeed the entry to the supply office, but that knocking on the door was totally forbidden. Entry had to be arranged by calling a number given on the door. I made the call.

The call was answered and I happily announced I was standing outside the supply person's door, and asked to be let in. Silence followed. Eventually the person on the line told me that it was unlikely that I was standing outside his office, as he was in a call centre in India.

The person in India kindly offered to arrange entry to the supply office. I hung up and shortly after heard the phone ringing behind the door in front of me, followed by some fumbling of locks and the door opened.

I was eventually given my computer, but told that I had

_____

* For something I could have gone to the local computer store and purchased off-the-shelf. Same brand, same everything.

breached quite a few procedures. I was supposed to email the supply office and they would deliver the computer. No one it seems, is supposed to go directly to the supply office.

Nearly all technological requests at a university go through a similar process.[*] All requests have to be logged via email, so that a job number can be created. When the job is done, another email is used to confirm that the job request can be closed. Why? Simple really: The tech staff have to justify their existence by documenting the demand for their services, and their job completion rate is used to infer their efficiency.[†]

Should you happen to see a tech person walking through your corridor, while you can happily engage them in casual chatter,[‡] any attempt to get them to help you fix your PC or some such request, will be met with the inevitable: 'Can you lodge that request through the computer system?'[§] The tech person will then leave, walk back to their office, read your official request, arrange a time to fix your PC and 10 minutes later walk back to your office and the job can get underway.

Truly a model of documented and proven efficiency.

---

[*] Often going via a call centre in another country.

[†] There is no point in doing something unless it is noticed and recorded. Lecturers will very soon have to keep a log of every email they write. While we are on that topic, check the 'Sent' section of your email and divide the number of sent emails in the last calendar year by 365 (days). That's how many emails you sent on average per day. After doing this you may want to go have a lay down, or a stiff drink (or both).

[‡] They will always be happy to do this.

[§] Even if your computer system is down and all requests for help must be made on your officially assigned PC.

WHERE ARE ALL THE ADMIN STAFF?

In some universities, the admin staff are forever being relocated, presumably so that lecturing staff can't find them and ask them to do something. That distraction would get in the way of all the admin that needs doing.

Some universities take the relocation principle to its logical extreme and have all the admin staff housed in one building. One with no academics in it.

This building is usually well hidden (for example, in another part of the city) [*] and should an over-eager staff member happen to stumble upon it,[†] the card-only security doors will prevent any attempt at entering the building. Seriously, it is easier to get into a restricted military base containing a crashed UFO, than an admin building.[‡]

The one sure thing that can be determined from many years of exposure to admin staff is that they are not there to help you: you are there to help them.

Each week the admin staff will request that staff provide them with vast amounts of information: lists of publications, descriptions of degree programs for marketing brochures, that sort of thing. It is not clear why this information is requested as the typical university is permanently two years behind in the recording of publications[§] and when marketing materials appear they will

---

[*] Also quite true.

[†] Unlikely, as the name of the university won't be visible.

[‡] Sadly, I have only ever managed one of these. Would you like to see my pictures of the aliens?

[§] It would be less, but they don't have enough admin staff.

describe the 2012 version of the courses.[*]

Nearly all requests from admin staff to the academic staff are labelled 'urgent'. There is always a deadline to meet. While the admin staff will try to make the lecturer believe that this deadline is real and is somehow their concern, it is not (on either count).

The admin staff always assume lecturers will be slow in doing anything, so if they give you a day, you can safely take a week.[†] Or better still, don't do it at all!

My recommended strategy here is to say 'Yes', to whatever request the admin staff make of you, and to then do absolutely nothing. If the job is real, and urgent, you will get an email reminding you on the day that the job really needs doing. You should hold your nerve here and … still do nothing. Let the deadline pass and several days later you can expect to receive an email from admin saying that the information they requested from you is no longer required, as they have decided not to go ahead with that project anyway. Added bonus: the admin staff will think you are hopeless and won't ask you for anything ever again. If there is a downside I'm not seeing it.[‡]

This may seem like a heartless and mean thing to do, as some admin people are actually quite nice people,[§] but it is extremely common for admin requests to be cancelled after you have provided the requested information. For example, suppose admin want to (urgently, of course) know the numbers of students in

---

[*] This always happens. Well, not always. Sometimes it is the 2011 version.

[†] Very Star Trek. Ask a passing fan to explain that procedure.

[‡] I know a Professor who has such a reputation for being hopeless that no one ever asks them to do anything. No admin. No teaching. Nothing. The Professor is very, very happy (and very, very smart).

[§] Most are. It's not their fault.

your discipline who drop out after second year. Searching the same databases that the admin staff have access to, you meticulously track down each student meeting the criteria and compile a very nice list. You even add a couple of very smart graphs, and a few summary points* interpreting the key data. It only took four hours. No problem. Click 'Send' and off it goes.

Not once do you ask why the information was required. That would sound rude and confrontational. One thing you do not want to do is upset the admin staff, so always be polite and remember to apologise a lot.† What happens to that data? No idea. You will never find out, but presumably someone somewhere will read it, and the problem of vanishing second year students (both of them) will have been forever been put to rest. Or at least until next year when you get the same question, but now you can make even prettier graphs with two time points.

A MEETING OF MINDS

While the admin staff are the cause of many pointless tasks, the academic staff are usually more than capable of thinking up their own ways to kill a working day (or two), most obviously, through a vast number of meetings. These meetings will share many common characteristics: long, unstructured and essentially pointless. But you will still be expected to go, and if you are really unlucky, to participate. So *drink the Kool-Aid*‡ and here are some of the

---

* You are an academic. You can't help yourself.

† Begin all communications with the word 'Sorry' (i.e., 'Sorry for existing').

‡ For the younger readers, *Wikipedia* defines this as a figure of speech 'that refers to a person or group holding an unquestioned belief, argument, or

most common meetings you may be expected to attend.

STAFF MEETING

All staff are expected to attend the staff meeting for their discipline.[*] The purpose of such meetings is to fulfil the university requirement that staff meetings be held. Apart from that, no one has yet managed to determine why staff meetings exist. Nothing concrete is ever achieved since all the important decisions have already been made long before the meeting. More intangible outcomes, like improved collegiality, might be a theoretical positive outcome, but how likely is that from a two-hour drudge-fest?

Staff Meetings begin with the reading of the Minutes of the last meeting. These Minutes, detailing all the important action items from the last meeting, will in most cases have been compiled from a set of illegible notes just prior to the current meeting.[†] Staff will begin by scanning the minutes trying to think up excuses for why they haven't done any of the things they promised to do at the previous meeting. But not to worry, a failure to complete a task ('I haven't had a chance to do that yet') will be met with a collective shrug, and a request to provide an update at the next meeting.

After the reading of the Minutes, the routine is always the same, each person with a made-up job title, say 'postgraduate

---

philosophy without critical examination', which will be good advice for most of these meetings. Do read the rest of the Wikipedia entry while you are there. Conformity has its dangers.

[*] This includes the Head of Department, who will try to be somewhere else if at all possible. That's the reason a 'floating chair' gets to run the meeting.

[†] Probably late last night.

coordinator', or 'research convenor', will give a short report that not-surprisingly takes forever. Every detail of every email they have sent since the last staff meeting will be detailed, building to the conclusion that they've got nothing important to say, but they will provide a further update at the next staff meeting. Oh yippee! As bad as that sounds, what is even worse is the coordinator/convenor who *starts* their speech by stating they have nothing important to say, and *then* reporting on all their emails. Bad move: a small sense of hope is essential when listening to reports at a staff meeting (please let this have some purpose!).

Since the introduction of computer calendar systems it has got harder to think up excuses to avoid staff meetings. Your Head of Department can see from your electronic calendar that you are free, and your attendance will be expected.* Try as you might, you will attend a lot of staff meetings.

HEADS OF DEPARTMENT MEETING

One day you may find that you have accidentally (it would not be intentional) gone and got yourself made Head of Department, or dumped into some other 'senior'† role for which you are given an invitation to attend the Heads of Department Meeting. Most universities work on the very sensible idea (not really) that they will function more efficiently if they throw a loosely-defined

---

* You are advised to block out Monday mornings and all day Friday on your calendar (these are favourite times for meetings). Put down that you are doing fieldwork or something equally unverifiable.

† It may be called a senior position but it is not. Head of Department is generally seen by Senior Staff as a low level role. The university only recognises roles ranked Dean and above as having any meaning. Remember that when you apply for promotion.

collection of academic disciplines into a single college or faculty,[*] where they can be more than the sum of their parts. This state of academic nirvana might be realised through cross-disciplinary teaching, or possibly research. No one is clear on the details of how any of that might happen.

Each faculty restructure will be accompanied by the relocation of staff from offices in one building to another, so that they can be near the staff from the other disciplines in their new faculty. All that cross-disciplinary fertilisation requires proximity! This is such a good plan that each university will create new faculties with new combinations of disciplines every few years. This process usually restarts as soon as staff have settled into their new offices and in some of the most nomadic disciplines it is worth hanging onto the moving boxes.[†]

To make such innovative collaborations work, Heads of Department meetings will be convened and you will find yourself in a room with people you have seen wandering around the corridors, but never had any reason to speak to.

Sitting together at this meeting will not in any way improve on that situation. The differences between disciplines are invariably deeply entrenched. Perceived slights and accusations of favouritism will be brought up several times per meeting, as in

---

[*] This college or faculty will be given a name which sort of applies to about 50% of the Departments. The other 50% of departments are advised to keep quiet and go along for the duration, as their departments are currently 'under review'. No one will even notice if they just vanish.

[†] I once arrived at my office at 9 am on Monday morning (I said 'once', it's not something I make a habit of doing) and found two removal men emptying my office. The decision to move my entire department was made late on Friday afternoon and the memo telling staff about the decision was still being drafted.

the ever-popular 'Why does Department x get more staff than department y?'[*]

It is at this meeting that all the best gossip, and the worst ideas, are given voice. For example, the Dean will reveal, in strictest confidence, the latest campus gossip, and then casually outline a plan to merge two completely unrelated degrees into something that 'will be really exciting'.[†] Heads of Department will be asked to comment on such proposals and even though they will be mentally screaming about the sheer impossibility of such a merger and the total insanity of even contemplating such an idea, what comes out of their mouths will reflect another mental scream, 'Don't be an idiot, don't say anything to upset the Dean'. And so they will prevaricate, ask a question (in reply to a question – always clever) and hope that someone else steps in. They will. The Dean of Teaching and Learning, or possibly the Dean of Research, will say that the idea is a bold one and that the Dean's vision is an inspiration.[‡] Meetings will adjourn strictly on time, although 90% of the agenda will have been held over for next week: The Dean's gossip really was interesting.

RESEARCH COMMITTEE

The Chair of the Research Committee is either a moderately successful researcher,[§] who has been chosen for the role for their abil-

---

[*] It's usually because they have more students. How unfair is that?

[†] It will excite the Dean, no one else, but you will all smile and say 'What an exciting idea' and secretly hope that you don't get drafted into the resulting *Special Project Committee* (see below).

[‡] These guys really know how to keep in with the boss.

[§] But not a *really* successful researcher. They wouldn't be wasted on something as silly as this meeting.

ity to 'inspire others', or a person deemed to be a research leader by virtue of having once (or maybe twice) sat on the supervisory panel of a student who actually managed to complete their PhD.

If your committee has the inspirational research leader-type Chair, meetings will be infrequent and very short. The Chair will distribute a list of approved journals (i.e., non-predatory ones that someone actually might read), and a list of the main grant bodies. The message here is that studying these lists is the path to being just like the Chair: it's that easy to have a successful research career.

In reality, the Chair has absolutely no idea how they are going to improve the research performance of their Department, School, College or Faculty, so instead they position themselves as a 'gateway', or 'facilitator', helping others 'to maximise their potential'. If you translate all of that management-speak into English, is comes out as 'Person who uses the 'Forward (all)' command in their email software and adds the acronym FYI'.

Research meeting over, the Chair is off to finish their new Category 1 grant application.* The rest of you can now go get on with whatever it is you do, having been suitably inspired. Next meeting is scheduled for next semester, or possibly the one after that. It's not like the Chair cares one way or the other.

If you have a PhD supervisor-type Chair, meetings will be frequent and long. They will have no structure, but there will be plenty of stories about how the Chair has completed yet another PhD supervision.† The reality here is that they were third on the

---

* Some grants are 'better than others'. Don't ever think you are a successful researcher just because you have millions of dollars in grant funding, a $50,000 grant from the 'right' body is what really counts.

† Or endless tales about the university's forthcoming three-minute-thesis

supervisory panel and can barely recall the student's name, let alone what they did their research on.[*] The unpleasant truth that the student took about a decade to do a PhD that resulted in zero publications (but two conference papers!) and that the student is now sitting at home, unemployed and likely to stay that way indefinitely, will never be mentioned. Meetings fade out rather than ending: someone relatively smart will announce that they have another meeting to go to and everyone else (i.e., those who aren't swapping supervision stories), will also suddenly remember that they too have meetings,[†] and the sudden mass exodus two and a half hours after the meeting started will bring proceedings to an end.[‡] Same time next week everyone.

TEACHING & LEARNING COMMITTEE

You have just entered Hell.

These meetings will have a very detailed agenda, probably running to about six pages,[§] with each point numerically sequenced to three heading levels ('Item 1.1.1, item 1.1.2', etc.). Despite

---

competition. This is presented under the mistaken understanding that such a competition counts as doing research. They are fun, but that's all you can say in their favour.

[*] As Head of the Research Committee the Chair puts themselves on the panel of any PhD students likely to finish, whether they needed or not. Truth is they are never needed, but that doesn't stop them.

[†] Look at your phone, screw up your face and announce you 'Have to go, this is important' and hope that no-one notices that your phone never vibrated.

[‡] Actually it won't. The Chair and their devotees will adjourn to the on-campus coffee shop where they can meet up with some current PhD students.

[§] If the agenda is in a table printed in landscape format, you have my condolences.

the precision with which the agenda has been sequenced, the meeting will probably start with item 4, before moving to item 7 and then back to item 1. No one will see this as in any way odd.

The meeting will focus on things like the course learning objectives of existing degree programs, and the need to ensure that these match the latest government initiatives to make sure the university conducts 'quality teaching'.

Despite this noble aim, the committee will spectacularly fail to do anything that might in any way improve teaching at the university. For example, despite the intense focus on making sure that subject outlines are filled in correctly, it's not as if anyone from this committee will actually read the outlines,[*] let alone draw together all that information to offer any insights into what teaching is really being done. Here are some questions that your Teaching and Learning Committee will never address:

1. Why has the teaching on many subjects (some of them key subjects) been completely handed over to postgraduate students?

2. Why does over half of the assessment on some degrees consist of multiple choice questions?[†]

3. Why does the assessment on Subject x consist solely of four blog postings?[‡]

---

[*] Other than to check whether the subject learning objectives are correctly aligned with the course learning objectives.

[†] As Head of Discipline, I made the mistake of collating all the assessment tasks and their weighted values from every subject in the undergraduate degree. This is the figure I came up with (I have since seen far higher figures at other universities). No-one appreciated me bringing this to light.

[‡] This is a real example. I fully expect to one day find a subject that is assessed via Twitter comments. And why not? If an idea is important sure

94

SPACE COMMITTEES

I once worked at a University where space was so limited that staff were required to share offices. This was not a great way to work, and so I asked if I could use the office next to mine which had a nameplate on the door but clearly wasn't being used. This provoked a very strong reaction, where I was called some not very nice things and my general attitude (not for the first time, as if you couldn't guess) was questioned. It turned out that the office had been allocated to a professor, who didn't actually work at the university.

Never had, probably never would.

His was an adjunct appointment and he actually worked in another country. He had only ever been to my university once or twice to give talks, and he had certainly never used the office. Furthermore, as far as my Head was concerned, the adjunct probably didn't even know he had an office.

So why was he allocated an office in our overcrowded workplace? Simple really, he was a very famous academic (a living legend) and the university liked the reaction of visitors when they saw his nameplate on the door of his office.* That was more important than staff having a space to work in.

The Space Committee at your university would probably look on such an example as a good strategic decision, after all, it's not as if staff actually need offices. Sitting in at one Space Committee Meeting (I had run out of excuses for not attending), it was proposed – in all seriousness – that a single communal space for all lecturing staff with 'hot-desking' would be much more effi-

it can be expressed in 140 characters or less!

* You guessed it. My sin was that I didn't know who he was. Not my area.

cient use of university resources. The vision here was that in the university of the future,* staff will no longer have offices, instead there will be one very big room full of computers. The underlying logic here was that as staff actually spend most of their time in lecture theatres (see *When you assume …*), having an empty office for most of the day is clearly a waste of resources.

Fortunately, that idea was swiftly shot down.

Unfortunately, however, the next idea was even worse. Another member of the Space Committee questioned why staff would even need that one big office, since they could do all their work from home, with lecturing being done by video links. Further, given that all the students are downloading lectures, why do we even need a campus? The land alone is worth a fortune!†

Beware of Space Committees. Those ideas are coming to your university soon and think on this: virtual universities will employ virtual staff!

SPECIAL PROJECT COMMITTEES

Being invited to join a Special Project Committee reflects the esteem‡ with which you are held by your Dean, and/or your perceived availability.

Special Project Committees are convened to organise events, create new programs, research centres and other such worthwhile pursuits. They are invariably made up of members of several de-

---

* In this case, 'next year' was the future.

† I wish I was making these up. All these plans really happened and were only stopped by a series of very long memos detailing why staff needed offices, and the citing of accreditation standards. If your discipline has no such accreditation standards, you are in real trouble!

‡ Could additionally include the two words: Lack & of.

partments, so the first meeting, which will have been convened in order to develop the agenda for the second meeting, will consist of the members introducing themselves and the election of the Chair. The person who convened the meeting, probably the Dean,* will either make a fleeting appearance at the start of the first meeting, or not attend at all. Their sporadic return appearances at subsequent meetings will be to chastise the Committee for its lack of progress.

Needless to say, when the project is completed successfully the Dean will take all the credit, unless an even more Senior Staff member does so first.† If the project fails, the existence of the project will be forgotten by all except the Dean, who will say nothing until your annual performance appraisal is being done. What they say then won't be nice.

SECRET SPECIAL PROJECT COMMITTEES

Yes, these exist, but not officially, obviously. They are secret and the only way you will ever hear about these committees is if you are asked to join one.

As with an everyday Special Project Committee, your task will be to organise an event, create a new program or possibly even a research centre. The reason this committee is Secret is because that event/program/centre is such a mind-numbingly stupid idea that the Dean, or some equally out-of-touch Deputy

---

* If they open by saying they thought of the idea while they were in the shower, you are in real trouble. BTW, that's a real example.

† I know of one Dean who thought up a new research centre, got the funding, recruited the staff and built a brand new building to conduct some wonderful new research. There was a glitzy official opening with the Vice-Chancellor and other local VIPs. The Dean wasn't invited.

Vice Chancellor (probably, Engagement), will want total deniability should news of the plan make it to, say, a local journalist. A good case in point here is a committee I joined 'to identify staff who wouldn't be missed if they were to leave', or if that wasn't the exact title (no minutes were kept) that certainly was the gist of it all. The meeting revolved around a staff list and the use of several different coloured highlighter pens. I have also attended similar meetings where whole degree programs were given the highlighter treatment, my own was in a very nasty shade of pink. That was not a good meeting.

EXAMINATION MEETING

The basic purpose of an Examination Meeting is to ratify the various final grades and to make sure that the right people have by and large, got the right results. The process would be so much simpler if lecturers could simply give marks to the students in line with how much they liked them, but apparently that idea isn't a good one.[*]

While the purpose of an Examination Meeting is all very sensible, a couple of minor technical issues, nothing important you understand, have, … well how do I put this delicately?

How about this: Totally and utterly stuffed up the entire system.

Yes, that covers it nicely.

Here is the first problem. Examination meetings are usually

---

[*] Don't even think about suggesting this. Everyone will stare at you and the Chair will covertly make some notes on their digital device, and won't make eye contact with you for the rest of the meeting. Not that I know that for sure, obviously. Never happened to me. Definitely not me. It was some other lecturer-type. Not me.

run by the Deans of Teaching and Learning who, as documented earlier, insist on *all* the results fitting a normal distribution pattern. There are no exceptions to this rule (even though the rule doesn't officially exist, which is kind of confusing). I know one discipline where the postgraduate students were graded as Pass or Fail on an applied task. Basically, they either got it right or they didn't. Elaborating further, they either did the task as successfully as a professional working in the field or they didn't. All was fine and good here until the Dean of Teaching and Learning got involved: having only two grades made a normal distribution impossible. The solution, the students all had to be graded on *how well* they had *correctly* done their work.[*]

Anyway, the desire to have *all* subjects achieve a perfect normal distribution is never official policy, but staff who want an easy life had better deliver the right numbers of students in each grade category. I recently saw this process taken to its logically absurd end. There was a subject that had four High Distinctions, when only three would have been expected if the subject had a normal distribution. The solution was simple: the student with the lowest High Distinction grade had their marks 'moderated' and they were given 84% (Distinction) instead of 85% (High Distinction).

If anyone else present at the meeting thought that was a bit off, no one said anything.

The other big problem with Examination Meetings concerns the timing, specifically, when they are held. In those golden days

---

[*] I would imagine that the question 'What is one plus one?' would also require a range of 'correct' answer grades. Perhaps the answer '2.00' would worth 100%, the answer '2.0' 75%, the answer '2' worth 65%', and so on.

of old, teaching would finish, exams would be held, then marked and an Examination meeting convened. After all due consideration, the results were released to the students.

Now, it is not unusual for the Examination Meeting to be held *after* the grades have been released.[*] Happily, at such meetings no one ever finds any problems with the grades.[†]

The problem here is that there are so many teaching periods in the year that there is always another teaching period looming, and the university want the students to get their grades so they can get some more of that quality teaching.

---

[*] You read that right. Re-read it again if in any doubt.

[†] If they do, they sensibly keep it to themselves.

8

THE LONG GOODBYE

PERFORMANCE APPRAISALS

Each year academic staff are required to document their achievements from the past year, and to outline their goals for the coming year. This document goes by many names, usually some variation of 'performance appraisal', and its stated purpose is to see how you are tracking as an employee and as such, the document ultimately becomes your report card.

While you are graded, curiously this is not in the micro-detail that would be used on a student assignment. Instead, your entire year will be reduced to a set of three words,* one for each of the main aspects of your work: teaching, research and administration. Officially, this is a constructive process intended to help staff to 'maximise their potential'.† Believe that and you will believe anything.

In reality, performance appraisals are a purely vindictive system designed to intimidate staff and to get them to do increasingly more work. Usually this means more teaching, or if you

---

* Sometimes four. The fourth word sums up the overall pattern from the three sub-domains of your work.

† Every time you hear that expression you know you are in trouble.

are really unlucky, more admin.* No good can ever come from a performance appraisal.

This can be proven with one simple question: how come staff with many years of perfect performance appraisals aren't automatically promoted? A string of excellent appraisals may be noted by a promotions panel (see *Promotion*), but they hardly constitute proof of anything, do they?

One of the reasons why promotions panels take so little interest in performance appraisals is because they recognise that the entire process is a living example of the maxim: garbage in, garbage out.

Basically, the questions you are asked in a performance appraisal are either inherently nonsensical, or sometimes inconsistent with the latest version of the university's strategic goals. For example, in the appraisal at one university I was required to explain how in the past year I had *personally* increased the number of domestic students attending the university, and as a follow-up how I would do even better next year. After explaining that I had personally gone out and press-ganged school-children into signing up at the university and that I would be expanding my recruitment strategy to target kindergartens, I thought I was on to a winner. The answer seemed to fit the university's recruitment goals and I was told that even though I had missed the neo-natal market, my methods were approved and I got a nice appraisal rating. Mission accomplished.

Unfortunately, over the next year the number of students applying to the Department was far too high† and in the next

---

* Apparently, there's a vacancy on the Space Committee!

† Can you believe it, a university admitting it has reached full capacity?

year's appraisal all the questions about recruiting more and more domestic students were missing. In fact, my answers from the previous year were now seen as counter-productive (obviously) and clearly, it was my fault that the Department was now in such a mess. Truly, there's no pleasing some people.

It should be noted that the questions in performance appraisals invite trouble. Here are some real examples.

• What you have done to improve the learning experience for your students?*

• What strategies have you used to encourage flexible learning? How have these strategies measurably increased the accessibility of your subjects/courses, and attracted more students to study your subjects/courses?

• Provide a brief summary of your contributions to the university's standing locally, nationally and internationally.

After spending a couple of days trying to answer such questions† you may start to question just what it is that you have been doing all year, as so much of it is hard to quantify.‡ A quick tip: list all the university events that you attended. Not

---

* Even though it was perfect last year, this year it has to be even more so. BTW, you will need to keep improving year after year, so it may be better to pace yourself. Report slow, but steady, year on year improvements and try to swap subject (or university) when you get to 100% satisfaction. After achieving perfection the only way left to go is down

† Remember you need to 'demonstrate' your actions: it's not enough to say you have done something, you must document and prove you have done it.

‡ I told you that counting your emails will be introduced one day. Remember, you read it here first.

only do these add some *demonstrable* content, failure to record them may result in a reprimand.[*]

One of the hardest parts of filling in the appraisal is deciding whether you can rely on the university's databases to auto-populate the appropriate content. I know one colleague who didn't cut and paste their teaching evaluations into the appropriate boxes because they believed the auto-populate would take care of that. Apart from the statement at the top of the page saying 'The data for this page will be auto-populated', it is difficult to see why my colleague reached such a crazy conclusion. Silly naïve fool! Of course the auto-populate failed and my colleague's blank teaching evaluation was recorded as 'Below satisfactory', even though the student evaluations had been excellent.

So how did that grading get decided? If the data is missing, the appraisal team work on the assumption that it doesn't exist. My colleague appealed this review but was told that 'the panel had been consistent in their interpretation of the evidence' and so it wouldn't be changed.[†]

I have a far worse example from my own experience. I had filled in my appraisal forms detailing all the grants I had applied for in the last year. I didn't trust the auto-populate facility (with good reason) so I made sure I covered all the bases with some diligent cutting and pasting.[‡] However, in my review the pan-

---

[*] I once missed the student graduation ceremony. I was on sick leave after an injury. The panel duly noted that I had failed to complete a required duty. I confess, I am a bad lecturer: I tripped over and broke myself. I promise I won't do it again.

[†] How very fair that is. Consistency is important, even when someone is wrong, being repeatedly wrong makes them consistent, which is a good thing, I think.

[‡] It is amazing how much time at university is spent doing the grown-up

el asked why I hadn't applied for any grants? I said I had and showed them the details of the applications on my appraisal form. I was then told that 'some lecturers lie about such things', so the panel could only accept that I had truly applied for grants if the university database confirmed it. In other words, if the auto-populate said it happened then it did. If the auto-populate showed nothing, then it hadn't. In this case, the auto-populate had shown nothing.

After being indirectly accused of lying (I thought it was direct, but an objective recording would show it was cleverly phrased to be indirect: 'Some lecturers ...' etc.), I went back to my office and pulled out the officially recorded (complete with code numbers etc.) and signed documentation showing the grant applications were real. I took this back to the panel who, with straight faces reminded me that this proved nothing as the auto-populate hadn't located those applications.

Determined to win this argument, I contacted the grants office to request an official letter acknowledging that the grant applications were real. They would happily provide this as they had received numerous such requests in the last few days. Apparently the grant application database wasn't linked to the performance appraisal database, so the auto-populate couldn't possibly work.

Slam dunk time. Got them now.

I went back to the panel, who thanked me for the information, but as I had already used up my one permitted appeal of their review that the assessment was locked in. Without any regard to the above events, the panel recorded that my failure to

---

equivalent of cutting up pieces of paper and sticking them onto some object or backdrop to create a piece of art. At least at school you could get a gold star!

apply for external grants was a serious problem and that I had better start applying for some next year, or else. To help me meet the targets, the panel suggested I should be put on a remedial performance plan.

I thought they were kidding. They weren't.

PERFORMANCE IMPROVEMENTS

Even if you pass your performance appraisal with the very best set of ratings (e.g., Superior, Superior and Superior) you should still expect the appraisal committee[*] to make suggestions about how you could improve.[†] Which is very nice of them. However, this invariably consists of advice to 'go get a postgraduate teaching qualification'.[‡]

Other ways to improve performance usually centre on attending many of the training courses on offer at the university. At the start of every semester your university will send round a list of training opportunities. You will be expected to attend some, so try to pick ones that are short, rather than based on an assumption that they will be in any way relevant or useful. None will live up to their billing and most run for a full day, some even longer.[§]

A good example here is a course run at one university to help women to be successful in their promotion applications. The

---

[*] Usually your Head of Department and one other 'neutral person' such as the Head of another Department.

[†] It will almost certainly be on your own time, and your own dollar.

[‡] When I finished university the careers advisor would say to every student 'Have you thought about going into accountancy?', no matter what degree they had done. The postgraduate teaching qualification suggestion is a bit like that.

[§] Avoid those. They probably take the roll so there will be no escaping.

course began by acknowledging that most of the women at the university were stuck at either the Lecturer or Senior Lecturer level. Given that starting premise, what then followed makes very little sense. The course focussed on how to get promoted to *Professor*, which none of the women in attendance was attempting to do (at least not in the short term).

Determined to press on, the course organisers brought out a set of real promotion applications that had been successfully used to get staff promoted to Professor. These successful applicants all shared a common set of characteristics: all were relatively young, their careers had never been interrupted by having children or part-time positions, category 1 grants had been rained upon them from the moment they finished their PhDs, and perhaps most worryingly: every single example featured a man.

On the plus side, that very same university later that year won a much-coveted 'employer of choice for women' award, just as they had done almost every year since that scheme was started.[*]

PROMOTION

In a sensible organisation, several years of outstanding annual performance appraisals should see you being summoned to the Head of Department to receive the news that your employer recognises your contribution, and you will be promoted a grade.

This never happens in a university.[†]

---

[*] I am beginning to sense a pattern in all this award business but can't quite put my finger on what it all means. No doubt I'll get it eventually.

[†] The only time this ever happens is when the lecturer has been offered (or is likely to be offered) a job at another university, say after winning a $500,000 category 1 grant. In such circumstances the annual promotion

Your chances of getting promoted are slightly lower than winning the national lottery. Reality check: no one at your university values anything you do and even though you will submit a 50+ page document detailing your numerous achievements, you will not be promoted.[*] That all sounds terrible, but it's a basic rule of university life that if you do something right, no one will notice: no one ever says 'thank you' or 'well done'. It is assumed that you will do your job correctly.

On the flipside, if you do your job badly, you can expect to receive a lot of attention. Bad news travels fast. As I am sitting here typing, an email has just popped into my account stating that the Head of Department for some discipline I have no contact with, has just 'stepped down' from their role to 'concentrate on their teaching and research'.[†] There's very little in the way of sub-text here, it's all pretty transparent, the Head has just been fired and has gone back to being just another staff member. This news has been circulated to all staff, even those with no possible connection to the department or people concerned. How very thoughtful.

Anyway, should you have the right performance appraisals, the support of your Head of Department and Dean,[‡] you might as well start filling in the promotion forms. In this application

round and application procedures go out the window. Now you know why your colleague got that surprise promotion!

[*] Not unless your demographic profile matches the demographic profile that the university has failed to recognise for promotion over the last decade and someone external has just spotted it.

[†] And probably gardening.

[‡] The unholy trinity for a promotion application. If you have all three, then your chances of getting promoted are well and truly stuffed. Sorry, not one of those things counts one iota.

you have to document all your teaching ratings, research outcomes, administrative brilliance all over again. But this time you have to do it in a form designed by a 9-year-old[*] that asks you, for example, to input each and every one of your achievements into badly aligned cells.[†]

The way	This works is to have you input the details of something, say	Your publications	One	At	A time into each row and column. You cannot adjust the cells, rows or columns so some sit there empty while you squeeze all the important stuff into a single cell. This cell always ends up being split across two pages.
Obviously	This is a nightmare if	Such as multiple	Because each detail, such as	Volume and issue, goes in	A different cell to page

---

[*] Obviously, a below-average 9-year-old.

[†] At some universities this form will be auto-populated from your inputs into the university register of publications/grants etc. However, these are NEVER up to date so you will still end up manually entering every publication, every achievement.

	you have a lot of achievements	publications.	the		numbers. Copying over your CV is going to be a couple of days' work. Add to that another day to make sure the rows align correctly.

No wonder it is easier to simply send the same core material (without the bad formatting) off to another university and to try your chances there. Good luck!

SACKING

Staff are rarely sacked by universities. Instead, the university always finds a way to get the staff member to resign. Sometimes this is through cruel and unusual treatment, which basically constitutes the *standard operating practice*. Occasionally, though they gently encourage staff to leave and provide them with the most ludicrously over-the-top endorsements that make the next institution think it is getting a superstar. Presumably that deceit only works once per welcoming institution?

The standard operating procedure to encourage resignation usually starts with a bad performance appraisal. This is sometimes quite difficult as some (unwanted) staff have managed to do all their assigned duties well, and there's not a lot they can be faulted on. In such cases, the solution is simple, either drill-down deep into each of the apparent successes and keep going until you find dirt,* or simply invent problems. I know of a colleague who was blamed for the bad teaching evaluations of a subject, which confused them as they hadn't actually taught that subject. The lecturer eventually found out that they had been incorrectly listed as the lecturer on a database, and armed with this apparent proof, appealed the bad teaching evaluation.

Never one to be deterred from a conclusion, the university simply blamed the lecturer for failing to spot that they were incorrectly listed as teaching that subject.† They even put the lecturer on a performance improvement plan‡ to improve their teaching.§

Whenever a university does go about forcing out a staff member, not surprisingly, it disguises its actions. I recently saw a group email sent by a Senior Staff member of a university, it started, 'The University has recognised the need to function more effectively to improve delivery and the quality of teaching and research'.

Almost sounds good doesn't it?

The email continued, 'A change in staffing expertise is required to meet these imperatives'. I was beginning to get a sinking feeling about this email and sure enough, what then followed was a list of academic staff positions that would be made redundant, and a list of several fixed term positions that would not be renewed.

---

* Or at least something that might look like dirt, if you close your eyes and put a bag over your head.

† The lecturer was negligent in failing to look up the subjects and find that they were incorrectly listed. If you need to go have a laydown about now, go for it.

‡ The university equivalent of being made to sit in the corner facing the wall.

§ I really wish I was making all this up.

This email bears some consideration. It starts with the apparently noble aim of improving the delivery and quality of teaching and research, which it then says will be improved by the sacking of quite a few staff members. Those guys must really have been *below average* performers if the delivery and quality of teaching and research will go up in their absence!

THE LONG GOODBYE

Once you decide that it is time to go,[*] you give your notice and then get to hang around doing nothing very much for the next few months.[†]

During this limbo period you can usually get quite a bit of research writing done, what with you not having much else to do. As productive as this period is, don't actually submit any articles to journals. If you do, they will not be recognised by your new institution as being theirs. However, if you really can't wait, then make sure you list yourself as having two affiliations (current and future universities) and that will keep everyone happy,[‡] especially you if your new university allocates money to your research account for every article you publish,[§] provided their name is listed as the affiliation.

While you go about your final days, it may strike you as odd

---

[*] Or it is decided for you.

[†] Especially if you hand in your resignation when you know there are no classes to teach for the next few months. Early December is usually a good time for resigning. If your contract should keep you there into semester 1 there's no way you will be assigned any teaching.

[‡] Except anyone with any integrity. This is a form of cheating, but no one will notice.

[§] This system is as close as you will ever get to a performance bonus.

that you are being asked to hang around for so long. Long ago, when a staff member resigned, they had to give about a semester's notice, and that would give the university a reasonable chance of arranging a successor. Even if the incoming lecturer also had to give a full semester's notice, a swift hiring decision meant that a very neat one-out, one-in revolving door system would ensure that there were no significant gaps in teaching.

As simple and clever as that system was, the new one is even better and goes something like this.

1. Lecturer hands in resignation letter.

2. Lecturer hangs around (3–6 months) doing as little work as they can realistically get away with.

3. Lecturer has lavish going away party at top local restaurant* and leaves. If the lecturer is still on speaking terms with the Dean, they may be asked to register as an adjunct appointment. This will mean that the university will get you to do work (like supervising PhD students) without having to pay you, and they will try claiming any of your future publications as their own.

4. New semester starts, Dean tries to calculate whether existing staff can cover for lost staff member (two months). Workloads are shuffled and Head of Department interrogated as to whether staff are *really* working to the specified capacity.

5. Dean asks Head of Department to prepare business case for hiring replacement lecturer (one month).

---

* You have to dream.

6. Dean grudgingly decides a new lecturer is necessary. Drafting of advert begins (one month).

7. Advert submitted through 'channels' for approval (two months plus).[*]

8. Advert placed (two months).[†]

9. Selection panel meets and interviews candidates (two months).

10. New candidate accepts, resigns current job and moves to new university (3–6 months).

As you can see, the process for hiring a new staff member is surprisingly long and torturous.[‡] This begs the question as to why the university doesn't start the process as soon as the initial staff member submits their resignation? The answer is simple: money. All the time that the university avoids hiring a replacement lecturer, the salary allocated to the Faculty can be spent on other *things* (its rarely ever spent on the Department affected by the staff loss). With minimal effort, a Dean can save well over

---

[*] I recently saw a job advert where the university had accidentally uploaded the job description and all the accompanying internal paperwork for the position. Ooops. I couldn't help but read it. The time between each of the three signatures required to get the job advertised was one month per signature. The initial call for the position had stated the new person was needed urgently as accreditation was on the line. Good to see everyone with signing powers appreciated the urgency of the situation.

[†] The length of time an advert is 'live' indicates how serious the university is about finding a quality candidate. If it's 2–3 months, then they are very serious about finding the best possible candidate. If it is next Wednesday, then the university has already decided which of the lucky postgraduates is suddenly going to be offered a Teaching Fellowship.

[‡] All good things come to an end; but really bad things seem to go on forever.

$100k through this stalling process, or even more if the outgoing person is a more senior member of staff.

In an ideal future department, all the staff will have resigned and teaching done by junior casuals working for a minimum wage.

In an *even more* ideal future department, all the staff will have resigned, even the casuals, and the teaching done through video recorded lectures.[*]

Think about that the next time you give a lecture and it is recorded, and remember 'What we do in life echoes in eternity'. It probably does.[†] Though that wasn't quite what we had in mind though when we started down this career path. It was meant to be somehow, more glorious.

Seeya.

SL

---

[*] As recorded in the preceding the year by the now departed Lecturing staff.

[†] It certainly does if it is a recorded lecture!

THE SECRET LECTURER WILL RETURN IN 'REVENGE OF THE SECRET LECTURER'

You can share your own experiences of university life (secretly, of course) at:

www.secretlecturer.com